THE LANDS
C
MORAY

SOME NOTES ON THE HISTORY AND PEOPLE
OF THE
BARONIES, ESTATES & LANDS OF MORAYSHIRE

Prior to 1850

Part 30

The Parish of Dyke and Moy
Prior to 1750

Bruce B Bishop FSA Scot.

No part of this publication may be reproduced, stored in a retrieval system or transmitted in any form by any means electronic, mechanical, photocopying, microfilming, recording or otherwise, without the prior permission of the Publishers
J & B Bishop

Copyright 2008 J & B Bishop

ISBN 978-0-9557032-5-6

First Published
January 2008

Published by J & B Bishop
Rivendell, Miltonduff,
Elgin, Moray

Printed by
Parchment (Oxford), Crescent Road, Cowley
Oxford

INTRODUCTION

The modern parish of Dyke and Moy was formed in 1618 by the combination of the earlier parishes of Culbin, Moy and Dyke, together with part of the lands of Darnaway. After this the main place of worship was in the village of Dyke, the church at Moy was allowed to fall into ruin and any possible remains of an earlier chapel at Culbin were buried beneath the sands.

The main route from Forres to Nairn and Inverness, having crossed the River Findhorn between Waterford and Moy, continued westward through the parish via Brodie. The Baronies of Cubin, Dyke, Darnaway and Brodie all held charters from the King and were allowed to the usual rights of Burghs of Barony such as holding their own markets.

The parish was entirely rural, the only settlements of note being Dyke, Kintessack, and Moy together with the settlements at the mansion houses of Darnaway and Brodie. Agriculture was the main source of income for the people, but in the east of the parish the River Findhorn provided employment for the salmon fishers.

The dates given against the pre-census inhabitants of the parish are those at which the person was known to be living in the area. Unlike many parishes studied earlier in this series, it has been difficult to ascribe places of residence to many of the people mentioned in the records, as this was not always identified, they just being recorded as 'in the parish'. This has led to the layout of the books being in chronological sequence rather than in geographical areas.

ACKNOWLEDGEMENTS

Acknowledgements are due to many individuals and organisations. Thanks go to Mr Graeme Wilson and his staff at the Moray Heritage Centre, and to the staff of the Historical Search Room at the National Archives of Scotland in Edinburgh. The Church of Scotland have kindly allowed the reproduction of extracts from the Kirk Session Minutes, and reproductions of extracts from the Seafield Muniments are by kind permission of Lord Seafield. Reproductions from other collections of documents are by kind permission of the National Archives of Scotland and the National Library of Scotland.

Early maps Top by Pont ca 1583. Bottom by Gordon, from Blaeu's Atlas 1654

CONTENTS

Introduction and Acknowledgements		page iii
Maps of the area		page iv
Contents		page v
Chapter 1.	Dyke and Moy Prior to 1618	page 1
Chapter 2.	Dyke and Moy 1618 – 1674	page 6
Chapter 3.	Dyke and Moy 1675 – 1699	page 24
Chapter 4.	Dyke and Moy 1700 – 1724	page 39
Chapter 5.	Dyke and Moy 1725 – 1750	page 58
Bibliography and Sources		page 73

Chapter 1

The Parishes of Dyke, Moy and Culbin before their union in 1618

The lands occupied by the early parishes of Dyke, Moy and more especially Culbin probably bore the brunt of various inundations of the North Sea. These were mentioned in the Red Book of the Priory of Pluscarden as happening ca 1010, by Boethius ca 1100, and by Fordun as quoted in Lord Hailes 'Annals' in 1266. Whether these were three separate events or just reiterations of the one catastrophe we will never know, but it is evident that the geography of the coastline of this part of Morayshire underwent dramatic changes. How this affected the early population is, of course, unrecorded. The vast quantities of sand deposited during this time, however, continued to spread over the land for the next 700 years, overwhelming much of the area with a deep cover of dry sand.

The present parish of Dyke and Moy was created from these three older parishes. These were the parish of Dyke with its church of St Andrew and Chapel of St Ninian; the parish of Moy, for a long time a prebend of Elgin Cathedral and joined with Dyke in 1618, and the old parish of Culbin where the settlement and ruined chapel had been buried beneath the drifting sands by about 1700. It is possible that at some early time the estate of Darnaway also held status as an independent parish, or may have been part of the old parish of Altyre. There were two castles in the parish of Dyke and Moy, these being Darnaway and Brodie, together with the mansion houses at Moy, Kincorth and Grangehill, the latter being eventualy renamed Dalvey.

The parish can be divided into eight main areas; to the west and north of the Muckle Burn are the lands of Dyke, including Dyke village, Brodie Castle, Cotterton and Downie. North of this, but still on the west bank of the Muckle Burn, lay the lands of Kintessack (sometimes referred to in old documents as Meikle Pennick), and at the northern edge of the parish the lands of Culbin, Earnhill and Kincorth. To the south and east of the Muckle Burn are the lands of Moy, and to the south of Moy are Dalvey, (also known as Grangegreen), Tearie and Earlsmill. The southern part of the parish is occupied by the lands of Darnaway, which include Whitemyre and Berryley. At the eastern edge of the parish there was a ferry boat across the River Findhorn, linking the village of Moy with Waterford in the parish of Forres.

Lesly, Bishop of Ross, in the 9th book of his "History" describes the village of Dyke as a "municipum", but no evidence of any municipal rights or privileges now remain, although there is documentary evidence that regular markets were held both here and at Darnaway. Even as recently as 1709 one of the main complaints to be presented to the Convention of Burghs by the Burgh of Forres was the fact that Forres was now surrounded, within two or three miles on each side, by the Burghs of Barony of Rafford, Altyre with its mercats at Blairs, Darnua [Darnaway] to the southwest and Dyck [Dyke] to the west. All of these had *"their own shoppes for retailing all manner of merchandise such as salt, iron, flax, mather, alum, spiceries of all sorts, indigo and all manner of things, and they also have severall mercats throughout the year and their weeklie mercats confirmed to them and punctually observed by the severall heritors and Chamberlains who send intimations far and near to repair to their mercats with horses, nolt, sheep, plaiden, linen, wool, timber and all other commodities"*. This was exacerbated by the fact that these Burgh of Barony markets, "*are customs free and therefore the whole country resorts to them so that few or none come to Forres, either to buy or sell, which has occasioned many of the inhabitants both of shopkeepers and craftsmen to turn bankrupts and diversly forced to beg their bread*".

The villages of Easter and Wester Moy were two separate settlements, the lands of Easter Moy, with their prebendary church and burial ground, were subject to the jurisdiction of the County of Nairn, because the lands had previously belonged to the Thanes of Calder [Cawdor] when they were the hereditary sheriffs of Nairn.

The castle of Darnaway was founded in the early 14th Century by Randolph, Earl of Moray, having a vast banqueting hall with an arched oaken roof, similar to that of the Parliament House in Edinburgh. Forming for a time the centre of administration of the powerful Province of Moray it was associated, before the Reformation, with the Dunbar, Douglas and Gordon families. In 1291, when the Comyns were keepers of Darnaway Forest, it is recorded that Edward I ordered Alexander Comyn to deliver to the Bishop of Caithness 40 oaks for the building of the roof of Dornoch Cathedral.[1]

One of the earliest recorded Charters was dated 26th January 1419, granted to Donald, Thane of Calder [Cawdor] of the Lands of Moy. James II is reported to have spent parts of two seasons at Darnaway in 1437 and 1460, hawking, trapping, spearing wolves and hunting deer with hounds.[2] On 26th June 1447 Archibald de Douglas, the Earl of Moray, was in residence at the Castle of Darnaway, as evidenced by a letter which he wrote from there to Alexander de Urcharte (Urquhart) regarding the lands of Urquhart and Darnaway. These lands, and many others in the area seem to have been part of the jurisdiction of the Earl of Dunfermline. On 29th May 1476 William, Thane of Calder, held the lands of Moy.[3]

In 1556 it seems that, in providing large quantities of timber for national purposes, much of the forest of Darnaway was devastated and that cleared areas were set aside for grazing, but later it was declared to be forest again. In 1562, following the Reformation, the imposing castle at Darnaway was acquired by the Stuarts and continued to be the seat of the Earl of Moray. Queen Mary held her court at the castle in 1564. Due to the densely wooded nature of the lands around the castle, partly in the parish of Dyke and Moy and partly in Edinkillie, the lands became known in many records as "The Forrestrie", a term used until the late 18th century.

Following the Reformation of 1560 there were a few years when many of the parishes did not have a minister, or the previous Catholic priest continued to serve as the Protestant minister. Until 1585-6 the parishes of Dyke and Moy were served by separate ministers. At Dyke Alexander Duff is noted as being the reader there from 1567 until 1585, and Andrew Simson was minister from 1574 until 1585. At Moy William Sutherland, the "Parson of Moy" before the Reformation, was deprived of his office in 1564 for refusing "to remove his kept woman". Andrew Simson, the minister at Dyke, then served both parishes until 1584, but Moy had its own reader, George Simson (possibly a relative) who served the parish until 1591. During the period just

---

[1] Phillips M T T, The History of the Ancient Oak Forest of Darnaway... Scottish Forestry Vol 55 No 3, 2001
[2] Anon. Royal Scottish Forestry Society 57th Annual Excursion, 1939
[3] National Archives of Scotland GD44/38/67/3.

following the Reformation, and at times during the next 150 years, much of the parish was recorded as being in the Bailiary of Pluscarden and the Regality of Farneen[4].

The removal of William Sutherland is recorded by Cramond[5] *"... for as meikle as it was complainit be the Commissioner of Moray upon William Sutherland, parson and exhorter of the Kirk of Moy, that he had not only disobeyit his charge commanding him to marie the woman with quhoum he befor had committit fornicatioun, but also had despyte the said Commissioner ryveing his letters of charge thereto, and had not obeyit his summonds chargeing him to compeir to this General Assemblie; in consideration of this despytefull ryveing of the Commissioners letters and also not compearing to this Assemblie, the Kirk depryves him fra all ecclesiasticall functions and also ordains the censure if the Kirk to proceed aganes him for his contempt."*

Despite this censure by the Protestant Church he retained possession of the Manse of Moy in the Chanonry of Elgin Cathedral, and was there from 1572 until at least 1588 with his *lemman* Isabell Crystesoun. The 'couple' had one daughter, Marion, but may have had several other undocumented offspring.

On 15th May 1584 Thomas Annand was appointed minister of Moy, but served less than one year in office. In 1586, at the time of the first suggestions of the union of the parishes, John Paterson was noted as being the 'Vicar of Moy'. In 1589 there are mentions of David Dunbar of Durris and his spouse Christian Falconer, and their son Mark Dunbar as holding the *"Lands of Grange Green and the Bogs, the Town and Lands of Moy, the Moy Land and the Newmill Croft"*[6].

A Charter by King James dated 6th May 1590 confirmed the status of Moy as the "terras Dominium et Baronia de Moy", effectively constituting Moy as a Burgh of Barony.[7] Part of the teind sheaves, however, still pertained to the Priory of Pluscarden. In 1592 William Dunbar was admitted as the minister at Dyke.[8] A Charter of the Lands of Moy was granted by Alexander, Earl of Dunfermline in favour of John Campbell of Cawdor.[9]

The estate of Darnaway was raised into a Burgh of Barony by a Charter of 1611, allowing it to hold its own markets and fairs, and to dispense its own justice except in capital offences. The Charter was renewed or reinforced in 1661.

Some of the inhabitants of Dyke and Moy before 1618

de Cawdor	Donald	1419		Thane of Cawdor, held lands of Moy
de Douglas	Archibald	1447		Earl of Moray at Darnaway
de Cawdor	William	1476		Thane of Cawdor, held lands of Moy
Sutherland	William	1564	1572	Parson and Exhorter at the Kirk of Moy
Duff	Alexander	1567	1585	Reader at the Kirk of Dyke

---

[4] National Archives of Scotland GD1/244/3
[5] Cramond. W. The Records of Elgin. Vol 1 reproduced in Fasti
[6] National Archives of Scotland GD44/38/67/1
[7] ibid
[8] National Archives of Scotland GD44/38/67/2
[9] National Archives of Scotland GD44/38/67/3

Simson	George	1567	1591	Reader at the Kirk of Moy
Simson	Andrew	1574	1585	Minister of the Kirk of Dyke
Annand	Thomas	1584		Minister of the Kirk of Moy
Dunbar	William	1585	1624	Minister of the Kirk of Dyke
Paterson	John	1586		Vicar of Moy
Dunbar	David	1589		Of Durris, held lands of Grangegreen
Dunbar	Mark	1589		Son to David Dunbar of Durris
Campbell	John	1610		Of Cawdor, held lands of Moy

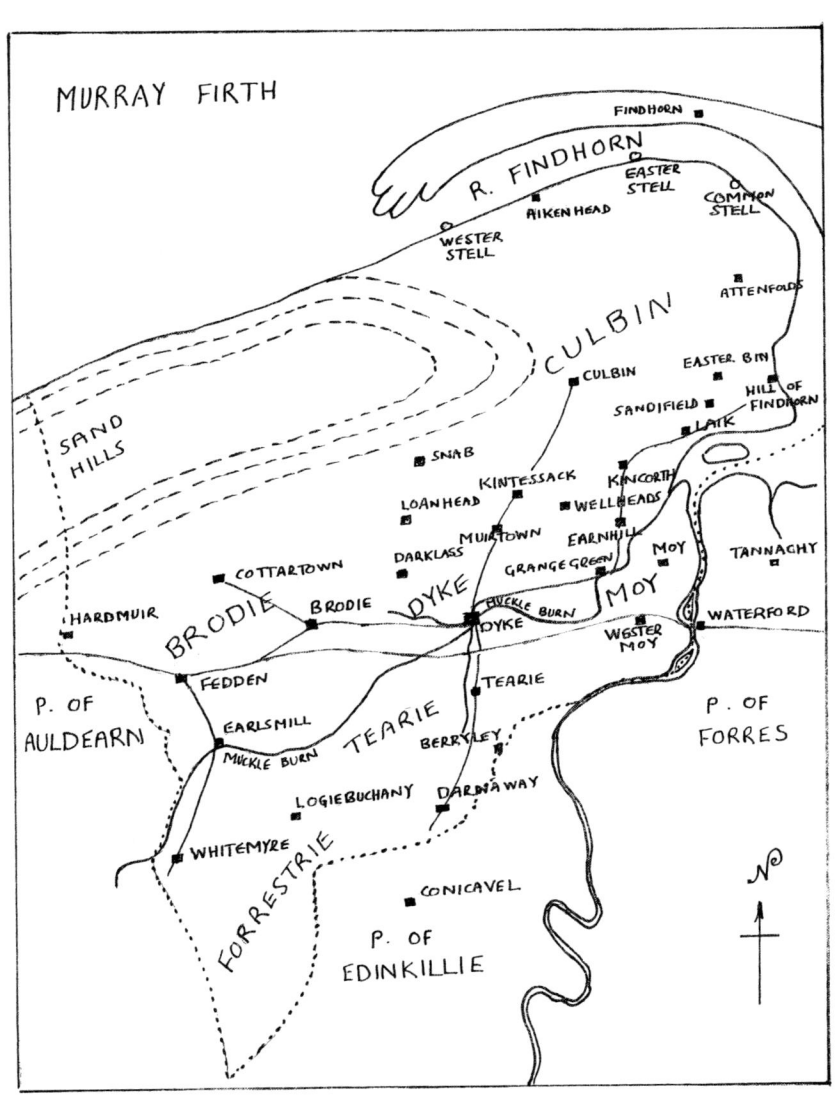

Sketch map of the parishes of Dyke, Moy and Culbin ca 1600

Chapter 2

The Parish of Dyke and Moy from 1618 to 1674

The formal union of the parishes was not completed until 1618, at which date the church at Moy fell into disuse. In 1618 William Dunbar became minister of the united parishes, and served the parish until 1624. In the decreet of union and annexation of the parishes of Dyke and Moy on 29th January 1618 there are mentions of Mark Dunbar and Hugh Falconer as Tacksmen of Moy, and William Sutherland as the Parson of Moy.

William Falconer of Kincorth was minister from 1625 until 1674. He was born in 1600, and married twice, firstly to Margaret Tulloch and then to Katherine Sutherland. The first manse at Dyke was built ready for his incumbency, and he died on 18th June 1674, still serving his parish.

On 2nd April 1635 the securities of St Ninian's Croft fell into the hands of Samuel and William Falconer, this was probably as part of the minister's stipend or lands. In 1641 there was a "Ratification of the Rights of Patronage of Moy and Dyck to Charles, Earl of Dunfermling". This further emphasizes the connections between the Regalities of Urquhart and of Moy and Dyke through the Earldom of Dunfermline.

The summer of 1652 was good, and there was an 'early and prolific harvest' with all the crops being in by the last day of August. The following year, however, was a complete contrast, the harvest was late, there were serious floods, and there was a 'great storm' in the autumn. On 27th December of 1653 there was another 'great tide and flood'.[10]

In the 17th century the majority of the population of the parish lived on the various estates mentioned above. Each estate contained a mixture of relatively low-lying fertile land ideally suited to the runrig system of agriculture in use at that time, and poorer land suitable for common grazing. Away from the residence of the proprietor, be it castle or mansion house, the remainder of the estate would have been made up of small 'fermtouns', held by a tenant, each fermtoun comprising maybe ten or twelve cottages in one of which the principal tenant and his family lived, the others being occupied by his numerous subtenants. These cottages would have almost invariably been of the 'but and ben' design, with one end of the building for the family, the other for the beasts.

Under the runrig system each of these cottagers would have had a small area of land adjacent to the cottage on which they were able to grow a few vegetables and keep hens and maybe a cow, and would also have held several strips of land, or 'rigs' in the common cultivated land. The strips held by each small tenant would not have been immediately adjacent to each other, but would have been spread throughout the lands, to avoid arguments and disputes about which tenant had the best and most fertile soil. The strips were generally about 150 yards in length, and maybe forty or fifty feet wide, sometimes laid out in a very open 's' shape. The space between each rig was uncultivated, often a home to stagnant pools of water, and full of weeds which seeded

---

[10] National Archives of Scotland. The Diary of Brodie of Brodie. T111.330

themselves amongst the growing crops. The beasts would have been led out to the hill lands each morning and brought back each evening, usually by the children, although sheep may have been left on the hill land throughout the summer, tended by men or boys living in the sheiling or hut on the hill.

A smaller proportion of the population lived in the hilly southern part of the parish on the estate of Darnaway, where the possibilities for runrig farming were more limited, except in the narrow valleys of the burns. Most of the crops would have been cultivated in artificial, often temporary 'lazy beds', or in small areas of land associated with each cottage. Hill farming, forestry and quarrying would have been the principal occupations of those living in these southern parts.

In 1653 William Falconer, the minister, preached against those who left his kirk to hear any other, and a Mr Laird complained that he was not edified by his (Mr Falconer's) sermons. The minister's complaint was probably a result of a rising tide of Episcopalianism, and neo-Popery, and the number of itinerant preachers now wandering the countryside. In the same year there are mentions of the Parish School of Dyke, and it was suggested that the children of families on the lands of Brodie should be encouraged to attend the school.[11]

In 1654 the forces led by William, Earl of Glencairn, in support of King Charles II were garrisoned at Brodie and Darnaway.[12] The old castle or mansion house of Brodie was severely damaged by fire at this time at the hands of Lord Lewis Gordon, and many of the old documentary records were lost. Some of the remains of the old structure were retained, however, when the new Brodie Castle was built.

In 1655 there was a meeting at Dyke "*anent the business of the Shire*", at which the Laird of Brodie commented that he had "*received much gross wickedness and obduredness*" and "*mourned the great abounding of profanity, uncleanness, drunkenness, lying, perjury, swearing, Saboth-breaking, ignorance and impenitence… which is in this place*".[13] All of this no doubt in support of the minister's worries of the previous two years.

On 23rd March 1655 the smithy at Brodie was burned down, and the smith (unnamed) received serious burns to his feet. The 4th to the 6th April of that year were "rough cold days" during which the English troopers were at Brodie, and the death, during the evening of the 14th of the same month, of John Willand, the servant to Brodie, was sadly lamented by the Laird. The 23rd April saw a visit by the Presbytery to Dyke to advise whether the people of the parish should pray for the King.[14]

The 17th May 1655 saw a meeting concerning whether the Kirk Sessions of the Presbytery [of Forres] should consider putting away "loose women" by transporting them to Barbados, and also the problems being encountered in providing aid to the poor.[15]

---

[11] ibid
[12] ibid
[13] ibid
[14] ibid
[15] ibid

The Laird of Brodie seems to have an interest in witchcraft, or at least in how certain women came to be accused of the sin of witchcraft. Cathrin Henrie, a suspected witch, told the laird how "*Sathan approached her somtyms in the shap of some friend, or her brother, sometym in the shap of a catt with burning fyri eys...*" The Laird of Brodie felt a desire to help her, and on 1st of November a day of prayer was held for her. On 26th of the same month John Layng in Dyke died.[16]

The 5th July 1655 saw further rain and another great flood, these increasingly severe weather events presaging the gradual decline into the very severe weather of the last decade of the seventeenth century. During October 1655 a motion was passed for the appointment of a new schoolmaster. John Laird, probably the Mr Laird mentioned a couple of years earlier, died in the stank behind Wightman's Hill, and Colin Campbell died on the same day. During the three days from December 10th to the 13th there was a great storm of snow.[17]

In early 1656 the Laird of Brodie was disturbed to hear that the King "*was turned Papist*". On 26th January there was yet another great flood, which was to be followed by "*swelling tempests and rains all year*". On 15th May the Laird of Brodie felt in necessary to admonish the minister, William Falconer, over the reporting of three prophane ministers. The next week Elspet Fraser was accused of witchcraft. In June there were still English soldiers at Brodie, and they were suspected of the theft of £30 which vanished from the house. The troops also proposed to take in all the arms in the parish, to avoid any possibility of an uprising by the local people.[18]

On 1st September 1658 there was again a great flood, followed by another in July of the following year. The weather had improved somewhat by 1662, and the Laird of Brodie described it as "*The fairest summer that has been seen, we had not ani storm or cold til the 12 of November 1662*". On the 2nd November the Brue House of Brodie was burned down.[19]

In 1663 Robert Milne, Katharen Lyon, Jhon Smith, Margaret Cumyng and Andrew Gordon were all censured by the Kirk Session "*for drinking on ye day of the Sacrament*". At this time John Stewart, "*a hopefull young man*" was called as the Schoolmaster and Session Clerk of Dyke.[20] During April of that year the jealousies between the Laird of Brodie at Brodie Castle and the Earl of Moray at Darnaway came to the surface, and were much commented on especially in the diaries kept by Brodie. David Hay, a servant to the Earl of Moray and a man seemingly much respected by Brodie, died on 6th April 1663. Later that year Isobel Elder and Isobel Simson, both convicted of witchcraft, were burned at Forres, much to the disquiet of the Laird of Brodie, who seemed to have sympathy with these women, feeling them to be misguided rathers than sinners. On 10th June the people of Earlsmill were raising disturbances due to their arguments about the marches of their lands, and just eight days later James Buchan and his son were drowned at the Monks Pier. This pier was

---

[16] ibid
[17] ibid
[18] ibid
[19] ibid
[20] National Archives of Scotland, Dyke Kirk Session Minutes CH2.779/1

probably in the vicinity of Binsness, and may have been so-named because it provided access to the Abbey at Kinloss just across the Findhorn.[21]

In 1664 the Kirk Elders and heritors were identified as Sir Robert Dunbar of Grangehil,l the Laird of Cubin yngr., Patrick Dunbar, John Anderson and John Duncan. The Poor List for this year contained 35 names, almost half of them in the village of Dyke.

In 1666 Alexander Cowie was censured by the Kirk Session for drinking "*the Session having found many other gross faults in him*". The Kirk Elders at this time were John Anderson and James Duncan in Dyke, and also William Gillan and William Watson. John Falconer received a public rebuke for having Mary Bell in his house, as she had been excommunicated, and James Hamilton "*a good hopeful young man*" was being considered as the new schoolteacher. Robert Glas and James Geddes were summoned for cutting some of the trees in the Kirkyard of Easter Moy. George Bardon in Moy, John Glas and James Lyons elder and younger were all censured for fishing for salmon on the Sabbath.

1667 saw Elspet Falconer, the spouse of John Cant, profane the Sabbath by "*striking her nibor woman*" and making many other slanderous expressions against her. The neighbour was not named but was identified as the wife of James Dunbar. Patrick Dunbar of Esterbin was ordained to pay to John Stuart the sum of £15 which he had borrowed from him as Session Clerk. James Smith, who had fallen into adultery some 16 years previously, and then fled the parish, returned of his own accord and was accordingly censured by the Kirk Session, who after all this time had not forgotten about his earlier misdemeanours. James Dunbar, the brother of Patrick Dunbar of Esterbin was appointed as a Kirk Elder, as were James Dunbar and Alexander Lie.

On 21st June 1668 "*taking to consideration the great necessitie and want of the poor and needy in the parochin; and great scarcity of birmeal in the countrey, they* [the Kirk Session] *thought it most convenient for supplementing them to buy some birmeal and to distribute it among them, therefore they ordainit for the minister and the former collectant William Dunbar to go up to Earlsmiln and buy six bolls of My Lord Murray's birmeal...*". This was distributed amongst the poor the next day.

In the same year the Kirk Elders were William Main in Darnaway, John Dunbar in Kintessack, and also John Duncan and John Hendrie. They also acted as collectors of funds for the poor. Isobell Miller made a complaint against Barbara Bell for slandering her and calling her an adultress and John Blackie profaned the Lord's Day by beating his neighbour.

It is often difficult to be specific about which part of the parish individual people lived in, especially before about 1670, and many of these people are just identified as being "in the parish".

On 14th January 1671 there was a great storm of wind and rain. In the spring the Presbytery met at Dyke "*for the trying Mr Jhon Falconer... he seemed to have some measur of knowledge and fitness*", this no doubt for the position of schoolmaster at

---

[21] National Archives of Scotland. The Diary of Brodie of Brodie. T111.330

Dyke. On 19th May the Lords of the Circuit held court at Darnaway, this being one of their regular, probably annual visits, to try any cases deemed to be too serious to be tried by the Courts of Barony or the Courts of Regality where local justice was usually dispensed. On 15th July trees were stolen from Brodie by Patrick Thom and William Laird in Dyke, they were caught and severely punished by the Laird of Brodie. William Dunbar in Brodie beat his wife so seriously that he was forced to flee to France to avoid punishment, where he became a soldier. On 30th August there was a meeting at Brodie about the *"rethacking of the Kirk"*, and John Ross and his wife Catherine Collace were reprimanded by the Laird over their continual arguments.[22] Also in 1671 James Geddes is identified as the Collector of Penalties for the parish, and John Mor, a poor sick pensioner was given aid by the Kirk Session. £1 was granted to James Fullerton, Student of Philosophie, as his parents were unable to maintain him at university.

On 15th January 1672 there was a meeting at Dyke between the Laird of Brodie and the Kirk Elders for the ending of the mortification of the Chappel-Croft, and on the same date the securities of St Ninian's Croft were disponed by Samuel and William Falconer or their heirs for the benefit of the poor. On 22nd March John Falconer, the recently appointed schoolmaster was given a warning about his neglect of his duties at the school, and on 29th of March the diary simply states *"This day Esterbin was buried"*.[23] This latter entry is very ambiguous, was this the funeral of the Laird of Easter Bin or was it the start of the burial of the lands of Easter Bin beneath the sand hills encroaching from the west? Janet Peterkin *"sustained poverty by the accidental burning of her house"* and Thomas Milne was given thirteen shillings aid when his house was also burned down.

"The gradual encroachments of sand have long continued to affect the neighbouring cultivated land, and a large proportion of the three Mavistoun Hills has been deposited in the north of the parish. The Barony of Culbin was most exposed, and the gradual encroachment led to diminutions of rent and population. It was only at the end of the [17th] century that the mansion house and gardens were overwhelmed, and the mansion house removed to Ernhill, the remaining corner of the Culbin estate."[24]

These problems later led to an Act of Parliament.[25] *"Act for the Preservation of Meadowes, Lands and Pastureages lying adjacent to Sand Hills"*.
"Considering that the Barony of Cowbin, and house and yards thereof, lying within the Shirriffdom of Elgin, is quite ruined and overspread with sand, the which was occasioned by the foresaid bad practice of pulling the bent and juniper, therefore His Majesty with advice and consent of the estates of Parliament... ... does strictly prohibit and discharge the pulling of bent, broom or juniper off sand hills..."

On 4th March 1673 the Laird of Brodie spoke to Colin Falconer, probably a relative of the minister, about William Falconer's neglect and shortcomings in his ministry and the possibilities of finding a helper for him. On 20th April the Council *"emitted an Act whereby all heritors were bound and lyable for private meetings in the bounds"*, probably referring particularly to those of a religious nature. On 22nd August the Laird

---
[22] ibid
[23] ibid
[24] Old Statistical Account for the Parish of Dyke and Moy
[25] K Will III 1 Par 5 Sefs Act XXX, Acts Vol 9 page 452 16th July 1695

of Brodie visited William Falconer, and in his illness the minister renounced Episcopacy to the Laird. On 18th August the Laird visited Greishop in the parish of Forres "*to see the harvest*".[26] Alexander Cowie, who had been censured by the Kirk Session for his "*habitual drunkenness*" was later returned to office at the request of the Countess of Murray. Precisely what this office was is not specified. Thomas Henrie and Isobell Mill were "*censured for drinking in an ailhouse on the fasting day after the Sacrament*", and also for their fornication. They "*confessed to their horrid guilt*".

In the same year there is reference to the 'Mortification of St Ninian's Croft' by the Minister, this being to the value of "*three bolls victual which [is] now for the use of the poor of the parish*".

On 11th January 1674 John Falconer, the schoolmaster, demitted office and George Kay, who was at that time schoolmaster in Alves, was "*admitted to be Schoolmaster, Reader and Clerk to the Session*" on 18th February, when he was "*formally chosen as Schoolmaster and to come to Dyke on Friday next to meet with the heritors*". The act anent burials of the poor was renewed on 26th April, and George Kay made his first appearance as Precentor on 3rd May. Following the death of William Falconer snr on 18th June 1674, his son, also named William Falconer, was installed on 20th September of that year, "*as none appeared to object anything against his entrie to the charge*".[27] He was married to Elizabeth, the eldest daughter of Alexander Tulloch of Tannachie, and was deprived of office on 10th October 1689 because he refused to read the Proclamation of Estates and also refused to pray for King William and Queen Mary. Following this he retired to live in Forres where he was known to be still alive in 1712. On 2nd August 1674 "*There was read publicklie ane proclamation directed from the Privie Council discharging conventicles*". What the extent of the Covenanters practices were in the parish of Dyke and Moy is unclear.

Also in 1674 James Bower in Wellhill gave in a complaint against Thomas Henrie in Kincorth regarding the violence by Thomas against Issobell Lie, the spouse of James Bower. Thomas was duly censured by the Kirk Session. An act was passed which required the Kirk Elders to sit in their own loft and not elsewhere in the kirk, and on 8th November and act "*required the masters of houses to ensure that servants from outwith the parish have sufficient testimonials*". Obviously the new minister was tightening up on church discipline. He also needed to keep a good roof over his head, and a notice was read "*anent the thacking of the kirk the next spring*". The manse was also in a state of disrepair, and an agreement was reached between the minister and the heritors over repairs to his home.

Some of the inhabitants of Dyke and Moy from 1618 to 1674

Dunbar	Mark	1618	Tacksman of Moy
Falconer	Hugh	1618	Tacksman of Moy
Sutherland	William	1618	Parson of Moy

---

[26] National Archives of Scotland. The Diary of Brodie of Brodie. T111.330
[27] National Archives of Scotland CH2/779/1/137-136

Falconer	William	1625	1674	of Kincorth, Minister at Dyke, renounced Episcopacy when censured for shortcomings in his ministry in 1673, died 18th June 1674
Fraser	James	1640		In Dyke, mentioned in Regality Court Book
Campbell	Colin	1655		In Dyke, died 27th October 1655
Laird	John	1655		In Dyke, died in the stank behind Wightman's Hall 27th October 1655
Layng	John	1655		In Dyke, died 25th May 1655
Willand	John	1655		Servant to the Laird of Brodie, died 14th April 1655
Buchan	James	1663		In Easterbin, he and his son drowned in 1663 at the Monk's Pier on Findhorn Bay
Cumyng	Margaret	1663		Censured for drinking on Sabbath
Gall	Margaret	1663		Censured for scandal
Gordon	Andrew	1663		Censured for drinking on Sabbath
Hay	David	1663		Servant to the Earl of Moray, died 6th April 1663
Lyon	Katharen	1663		Censured for drinking on Sabbath
Milne	Robert	1663		Censured for drinking on Sabbath
Smith	John	1663	1671	In fornication with Janet Oge, censured for drinking on Sabbath
Stewart	John	1663	1667	In Dyke, Schoolmaster, Session Clerk and Treasurer to Kirk Session
Anderson	John	1664	1670	In Kintessack, Collector and Kirk Elder, organized food distributions to the poor
Barber	Bessie	1664		In fornication with John Lambie
Bell	Margaret	1664		In adultery with John Watson
Brander	Isobell	1664		In fornication with William Williken
Bremner	Isobell	1664		In scandal with Alexander Lyon
Cumyng	Jean	1664		Excommunicated
Duk	Elspet	1664		In fornication with Thomas Paterson
Dunbar	George	1664		In fornication with Agnes Sutherland
Dunbar	James	1664		Censured by Kirk Session
Dunbar	Patrick	1664	1666	In Earlsmill, Heritor and Kirk Elder
Dunbar	Robert	1664	1666	In Grangehill, Heritor and Kirk Elder
Duncan	John	1664	1668	In Dyke, Collector and Kirk Elder
Falconer	Patrick	1664		In Earlsmill, abused by Bessie Marshall
Gall	Katharen	1664		In fornication with Duncan Smith
Hay	Alexander	1664		In fornication with Susann Ker
Keath	James	1664		He and his wife 'cursed' his mother
Ker	Susann	1664		In fornication with Alexander Hay
Lambie	John	1664		In fornication with Bessie Barber
Leslie	Patrick	1664		Servant to Bailie Brown
Lie	David	1664		In dispute over lands in Dyke
Lyon	Alexander	1664		In scandal with Isobell Bremner
Marshall	Bessie	1664		In Earlsmill, censured for abuse of Patrick Falconer

Mill	Robert	1664		Censured for fornication
Nicolson	John	1664	1671	In dispute over lands of Dyke, also censured by Kirk Session
Paterson	Thomas	1664		In fornication with Elspet Duk
Russell	Cristane	1664		In fornication with William Shippherd
Shippherd	William	1664		In fornication with Cristane Russell
Smith	Duncan	1664		In fornication with Katharen Gall
Sutherland	Agnes	1664		In fornication with George Dunbar
Thomson	Patrick	1664		Kirk Elder, organised food distribution to the poor
Watson	John	1664	1673	In adultery with Margaret Bell in 1664, given aid by Kirk Session in 1673
Aibel	Alexander	1665		In Chishill, on Poor List
Anderson	Isobell	1665		In Darnaway, on Poor List
Angus	Isobell	1665		In Culbin, on Poor List
Badon	Margaret	1665	1668	In Culbin, on Poor List, given additional firlot of meal in 1668
Barclay	Barbara	1665	1666	In Darnaway, on Poor List, given additional 6/0d aid by Kirk Session
Blackie	James	1665	1694	In Darnaway, husband of Bessie Murdoch, later on Poor List, and given additional firlot of meal in 1668. Died in July 1694
Blackie	John	1665	1678	In Grangegreen, Censured for beating his neighbour Alexander Blackie whilst drunk on the Lord's Day, later on Poor List
Brodie	Isobell	1665	1673	On Poor List, additional meal in 1668
Brodie	Katherine	1665	1671	On Poor List, granted testificat
Buchan	Isobell	1665		On Poor List
Burges	James	1665		In Darnaway, on Poor List
Cleark	Michal	1665		In Moy, on Poor List
Cowie	Elspet	1665		In fornication with John Paterson
Cunninghame	John	1665	1673	On Poor List, additional meal in 1668
Dolare	John	1665		A poor distressed man, aid by K S
Dunbar	Jean	1665	1667	In fornication with Walter Lie, fined 2/0d by Kirk Session
Dunbar	John	1665		In fornication with Cristan Murdoch
Dunbar	William	1665	1666	In Kintessack, Heritor and Kirk Elder
Falconer	Agnes	1665	1673	On Poor List, additional meal in 1668
Falconer	Hugh	1665		In fornication with Marjory Forsyth and with Margaret Leal
Falconer	John	1665	1666	In fornication with Elspet Cowie, and cohabited with Mary Bell, censured
Forsyth	Marjory	1665	1675	In fornication with Hugh Falconer
Fraser	John	1665	1673	In Kincorth, on Poor List
Gaa	Hugh	1665		In fornication with Ursula Lyon
Hardie	Andrew	1665		Beat and shook Isobell Paterson
Henrie	James	1665	1668	In Kincorth, on Poor List
Henrie	Marjory	1665		In Boghill, on Poor List

Herywood	George	1665	1668	In Earlsmill, on Poor List
Kemp	Isobel	1665	1668	In Cottartown of Brodie, on Poor List
Kynaird	Bessie	1665		In Kincorth, on Poor List
Leal	Margaret	1665		In fornication with Hugh Falconer
Lie	Walter	1665		In fornication with Jean Dunbar
Logan	Ann	1665		Servant to Earl of Moray at Darnaway, given permission to marry Jas Murdoch
Lyon	Ursula	1665		In fornication with Hugh Gaa
MacJames	Bessie	1665	1666	In Kincorth, on Poor List, given 4/0d additional aid in 1666
Marshall	Jean	1665	1668	On Poor List, 1 firlot additional aid 1668
Meft	John	1665	1673	On Poor List
Mill	David	1665	1673	On Poor List
Mill	Jannet	1665	1677	In Boghill, on Poor List, her winding sheet cost £1/1/0d in 1677
Mill	John	1665	1673	In Grangegreen, on Poor List
Murdoch	Cristan	1665		In fornication with John Dunbar
Murdoch	James	1665		Servant to Earl of Moray at Darnaway, given permission to marry Ann Logan
Paterson	Isobell	1665		Assaulted by Andrew Hardie
Porterfield	Katharen	1665		On Poor List
Pyper	Mary	1665		In Boghill, on Poor List
Rait	David	1665		In Grangegreen, on Poor List
Simpson	Isobel	1665		On Poor List
Tailzeour	Isobell	1665		On Poor List
Urquhart	Helen	1665		In Kincorth, on Poor List
Urquhart	John	1665	1673	On Poor List
Wilson	Margaret	1665	1673	In Darnaway, on Poor List
Wright	Isobell	1665		On Poor List
Wright	Walter	1665		In fornication with Janet Young
Young	Janet	1665		In fornication with Walter Wright
Angus	Isobell	1666		In fornication with John Pirie
Barron	George	1666		In Moy, fished for salmon on Sabbath
Bell	Mary	1666		An excommunicate person following a gross and flagrant fall from grace
Cuie	James	1666		In Darnaway, in fornication with Jean Fraser
Dunbar	Cristan	1666	1667	In fornication with William Dunbar
Dunbar	James	1666	1667	In Easterbin, Kirk Elder, brother to Patrick Dunbar
Dunbar	John	1666	1668	In Kintessack, Collector and Kirk Elder
Dunbar	William	1666	1667	In fornication with Cristan Dunbar
Edie	James	1666		In fornication with Isobell Falconer
Falconer	Isobell	1666		In fornication with James Edie
Fimister	James	1666		'A poor man'
Fraser	Jean	1666		In Darnaway, in fornication with James Cuie
Fraser	Jean	1666		In Dyke, witness against Mary Bell
Geddes	James	1666	1677	In Moy, Wright and Kirk Elder, gave bond to Kirk Session. Employed to cut

Glass	John	1666		trees in kirkyard at Easter Moy and build new bridge In Moy, fished for salmon on Sabbath
Glass	Robert	1666	1688	Employed to cut trees in kirkyard of Easter Moy, his Testament dated 1688
Hamilton	James	1666		A 'good hopeful young man' considered for post of Schoolmaster
Lyon	James jnr	1666		In Moy, fished for salmon on Sabbath
Lyon	James snr	1666		In Moy, fished for salmon on Sabbath
Meft	Isobell	1666		A 'poor distressed woman'
Mill	Hew	1666	1677	In Muryhill, in fornication with Marjorie Findlay, Katherin Roy and also Christan Pyper
Pirie	John	1666		In fornication with Isobel Angus
Pyper	Christan	1666		In fornication with Hugh Mill
Smith	Hugh	1666		Father of a child by Isobell Tulloch
Tulloch	Isobell	1666		With child by Hugh Smith
Watson	William	1666		Kirk Elder
Austie	Ursula	1667	1673	In Moy, in fornication with Donald Lyon in 1667 and with David Bremner in 1673
Badon	Alexander	1667	1674	Censured for repeated Breaches of Sabbath
Brodie	John	1667		Slandered by Andrew Glass
Campbell	John	1667		A poor man, given 6d aid by K S
Cant	John	1667	1671	Husband of Elspet Falconer, censured for fishing on the Sabbath
Clark	Margaret	1667		In fornication with Andrew Urquhart
Cook	Robert	1667	1676	At Mill of Moy,, gave bond to Kirk Session. 'Cursed' by Grizel Forbes
Crystie	James	1667		In fornication with Jean Fraser
Demster	William	1667		In fornication with Ester Lyon
Dunbar	John	1667		Fined 2/0d by Kirk Session
Dunbar	John	1667		A poor man in Dyke, given 4/0d aid
Dunbar	Margaret	1667	1672	In fornication with Alexander Pyper in 1667, granted a testificat in 1672
Dunbar	Patrick	1667		In Easterbin, Kirk Elder, repaid bond to Kirk Session
Dunbar	Robert	1667	1668	In fornication with Jean Lindsay
Dunbar	Walter	1667		In fornication with Margaret Mackie
Falconer	Elspet	1667		Wife of John cant, profaned Sabbath
Forbes	Grizel	1667		Censured for 'cursing' Robert Cook
Fraser	Jean	1667		In fornication with James Crystie
Glass	Andrew	1667		Slandered John Brodie, censured by KS
Kirk	Agnes	1667		A poor woman, given 6d aid
Lie	Alexander	1667		Kirk Elder
Lindsay	Jean	1667		In fornication with Robert Dunbar
Lyon	Bessie	1667		Desired marriage to John Walker
Lyon	Donald	1667	1673	In fornication with Ursula Austie and Elspet Waxter, also profaned Lord's Day and had absences from the kirk

Lyon	Ester	1667		In fornication with William Demster
MackGrigour	William	1667		Censured by Kirk Session
Mackie	Margaret	1667		In fornication with Walter Dunbar
Mitchell	James	1667		Censured for Breach of Sabbath
Pyper	Alexander	1667		In fornication with Margaret Dunbar
Shearer	James	1667		Censured for Breach of Sabbath
Smith	James	1667		Adulterer, fled parish in 1651, now returned, censured by Kirk Session
Urquhart	Andrew	1667		In fornication with Margaret Clark
Urquhart	James	1667		Censured for Breach of Sabbath
Walker	John	1667		Desired marriage to Bessie Lyon
Bell	Alexander	1668	1673	On Poor List, additional firlot in 1668
Bell	Barbara	1668		Called Isobell Miller an adultress, censured for slander
Brodie	Elspet	1668		On Poor List, additional firlot in 1668
Brodie	John	1668		In Longhill, in fornication with Elspet Martin despite being contracted to marry John Duncan's daughter
Brodie	Margaret	1668		On Poor List, 1 additional firlot of meal
Burrie	Alexander	1668	1673	On Poor List
Cadell	Katharen	1668		On Poor List, 1 additional firlot of meal
Clark	Barbara	1668		In fornication with James Cruich
Clark	Michal	1668	1673	On Poor List, 1 additional firlot of meal
Craig	William	1668		In adultery with Elspet Russell
Cruich	James	1668		In fornication with Barbara Clark
Dolas	Elspet	1668		'Gave ill language'
Dunbar	George	1668		On Poor List
Dunbar	Janet	1668	1673	On Poor List, 1 additional firlot of meal
Dunbar	Patrick	1668		On Poor List
Duncan	John	1668		In Longhill, his daughter contracted to marry John Brodie
Ferguson	Ursula	1668	1673	On Poor List
Gillan	John	1668		On Poor List, 1 additional firlot of meal
Gowie	Alexander	1668		In Kincorth, on Poor List, 1 additional firlot of meal
Grigor	Janet	1668		On Poor List, 1 additional firlot of meal
Hardie	John	1668	1673	On Poor List, 1 additional firlot of meal
Hardy	Isobel	1668		In fornication with Adam Lindsay
Hendrie	Isobel	1668		On Poor List, 1 additional firlot of meal
Hendrie	John	1668		Collector and Kirk Elder
Henrie	Katharen	1668		On Poor List, 1 additional firlot of meal
Jonston	Margaret	1668	1673	On Poor List, 1 additional firlot of meal
Jughill	Catherine	1668		On Poor List, 1 additional firlot of meal
Kynaird	Alexander	1668		In Kincorth, on Poor List, 1 additional firlot of meal
Kynaird	Elspet	1668		On Poor List, 1 additional firlot of meal
Lie	Adam	1668	1673	On Poor List
Lie	Angus	1668		On Poor List, 1 additional firlot of meal
Lindsay	Adam	1668		In fornication with Isobel Hardy
Main	William	1668		In Darnaway, Collector and Kirk Elder

Martin	Elspet	1668		In fornication with John Brodie
Meft	Jean	1668	1673	On Poor List, 1 additional firlot of meal
Mill	Elspet	1668		On Poor List, 1 additional firlot of meal
Miller	Isobell	1668		Complained to KS about Barbara Bell who slandered her as an adultress
Murdoch	Isobell	1668	1673	On Poor List, 1 additional firlot of meal
Murray	Margaret	1668		On Poor List
Nicol	James	1668		In Moy, fished for salmon on Lord's Day
Paterson	Jean	1668	1675	In Easterbin, in fornication with Robert Nicolson
Phimister	Janet	1668		On Poor List, 1 additional firlot of meal
Ross	Alexander	1668		On Poor List
Ross	Elspet	1668	1677	In Fedden, on Poor List, 1 additional firlot of meal in 1668, bedfast by 1677 and given 6/0d aid by KS
Russell	Elspet	1668		In adultery with William Craig
Russell	John	1668		In Boggs, on Poor List, 1 additional firlot of meal
Simson	Isobell	1668		On Poor List, 1 additional firlot of meal
Smith	Janet	1668	1673	On Poor List, 1 additional firlot of meal
Spens	Marjory	1668	1673	On Poor List, 1 additional firlot of meal
Taylor	Isobell	1668		On Poor List, 1 additional firlot of meal
Thomson	Margaret	1668	1673	On Poor List
Watson	Marjory	1668		On Poor List, 1 additional firlot of meal
Watson	William	1668		In Boggs, on Poor List, 1 additional firlot of meal
Wilan	David	1668		On Poor List, 1 additional firlot of meal
Wilan	Margaret	1668		On Poor List, 1 additional firlot of meal
Wright	Andrew	1668		On Poor List
Wright	Bessie	1668		On Poor List, 1 additional firlot of meal
Badon	John	1669	1674	In fornication with Jean Lyon, also censured for working on Lord's Day
Baxter	John	1669	1675	Servant to Earl of Moray at Darnaway, several times in fornication with Janet Lie
Lie	Janet	1669	1675	In Darnaway, several times in fornication with John Baxter
Lyon	Jean	1669		In fornication with John Badon
Falconer	William	1670	1676	Schoolmaster, admitted as Kirk Elder
Hardie	Jean	1670		In fornication with William Latto
Latto	William	1670		In fornication with Jean Hardie
Alves	David	1671		In fornication with Christian Strachan
Belyman	Agnes	1671	1673	In Earlsmill, in fornication with James Dick 1671, with Hew Falconer 1673
Bowie	Robert	1671		Censured for fishing on the Sabbath
Brabner	Marjory	1671		Censured by Kirk Session
Burnet	Elspet	1671		Granted a testificat
Collace	Catherine	1671		Wife of John Ross in Brodie, censured by Kirk Session for arguing with him
Cruickshanks	John	1671		Censured for fishing on the Sabbath

Dick	James	1671	1673	In fornication with Agnes Belyman 'his woman', also with Jean Vass in 1673
Dunbar	William	1671		In Brodie, beat his wife then fled to France to be a soldier
Falconer	John	1671	1674	Given trial as Schoolmaster in 1671, appointed, the reprimanded for neglect of his students, demitted office 11th January 1674
Fullerton	James	1671		Student of Philosophie, given £1 aid
Geddes	John	1671		Collector of Penalties
Hamilton	James	1671		Censured by Kirk Session
Laird	William	1671		Stole trees from Brodie estate
Milne	Hew	1671		Censured by Kirk Session
Mor	John	1671		Poor sick parishioner, given aid by KS
Murdoch	Bessie	1671		In fornication with William Sinclair in Forres
Oge	Janet	1671		In fornication with John Smith
Peterkin	Patrick	1671	1676	In adultery with Isobell Sutor, later granted testimonial for his move to Forres
Ross	John	1671		In Brodie, husband of Catherine Collace, censured by KS for arguing with her
Strachan	Christian	1671		In fornication with David Alves
Suter	Alexander	1671	1672	Fornicator, he and his son also censured for Breach of Sabbath
Sutor	Isobell	1671		In adultery with Patrick Peterkin
Taylor	George	1671		Given £1/12/0d by KS to buy a Bible
Thomson	Patrick	1671		Stole trees from Brodie estate
Young	Katharen	1671		Censured by Kirk Session
Anderson	Jean	1672		In fornication with Alexander Lie
Bell	Marjory	1672		In fornication with John Leal
Bowie	Alexander	1672		An habitual drunkard
Brebner	Thomas	1672		Censured for being drunk on Sabbath
Dolas	Isobell	1672		Granted a testificat
Dunbar	Alexander	1672		Given aid by Kirk Session
Grant	James	1672		An infirm old man
Hardie	Janet	1672		An infirm old woman, given 16/0d aid
Henrie	Thomas	1672	1674	In Kincorth, in fornication with Isobell Mill, assaulted James Bower's wife and censured for drinking in an alehouse on a fast day
Hutcheon	John	1672		An infirm old man, given 16/0d aid
Leal	John	1672	1674	In fornication with Marjory Bell and with Isobell Phimister
Lie	Alexander	1672		In fornication with Jean Anderson
Mill	Isobell	1672	1673	In fornication with Thomas Howie, also drinking in an alehouse on a fast day
Milne	Thomas	1672		House burned down, given 13/0d aid by Kirk Session
Moren	John	1672		In fornication with Janet Torrie 'his

Surname	Forename	Year	Year2	Note
Peterkin	Janet	1672		woman' House burned down, given aid by KS
Torrie	Janet	1672		In fornication with John Moren
Wright	George	1672		Drunk on Sabbath
Anderson	Moses	1673		In fornication with Marjory Thomson
Austie	Margaret	1673		In Earlsmill, in fornication for 3rd time with James Brown
Austie	Ursula	1673		In Moy, fornication with David Bremner
Barber	Katherine	1673		On Poor List
Baxter	Elspet	1673		Censured by Kirk Session
Bower	James	1673	1674	In Wellhill, on Poor List, gave in complaint against Thomas Henrie in Kincorth
Brabner	Thomas	1673		Given aid and a firlot beremeal by KS
Bremner	David	1673		In Moy, fornication with Ursula Austie
Brown	James	1673		In Earlsmill, fornication with Margaret Austie
Cowie	Alexander	1673		A habitual drunkard
Dick	Margaret	1673		On Poor List
Dunbar	Thomas	1673		On Poor List
English	Katherine	1673		On Poor List
Falconer	Colin	1673		In Brodie, Kirk Elder
Falconer	Hew	1673		In Earlsmill, fornication with Agnes Belyman
Findlay	Marjorie	1673		In fornication with Hew Mill
Henry	James	1673		On Poor List
McKenzie	Janet	1673		Received 4/0d aid from Kirk Session
Meason	Margaret	1673		On Poor List
Mill	Jean	1673		On Poor List
Murray	Katharine	1673		On Poor List
Nicolson	Robert	1673	1675	In Easterbin, in fornication with Jean Paterson
Phimister	James	1673		On Poor List
Pyper	Margaret	1673		On Poor List
Sinclair	Andrew	1673		On Poor List
Strachan	George	1673		On Poor List
Thomson	Marjory	1673		In fornication with Moses Anderson
Vass	Jean	1673		In fornication with James Dick
Waxter	Elspet	1673		In fornication with Donald Lyon
Alves	Thomas	1674		Paid £2 for binding the Session Book
Anderson	Bessie	1674		In Leyhill, very weak and poor, given aid by Kirk Session
Anderson	Christian	1674		Granted a testificat
Brodie	David	1674		In fornication with Isobel Man, he now gone to Thurso
Chrystie	James	1674	1693	In Darnaway, Chamberlain to the Earl of Moray, admitted as a Kirk Elder
Clunas	Margaret	1674	1675	In antenuptial fornication with David Smith
Davidson	Janet	1674		In Culbin, in fornication with Patrick

Falconer	William	1674	1689	Gordoune there Succeeded his father as Minister of Dyke, admitted 20th September 1674, deprived of office in 1689
Gordoune	Patrick	1674		Servant to the Laird of Culbin, in fornication with Janet Davidson
Gowie	Alexander	1674		Kirk Officer
Hardie	Elspet	1674		In fornication with John Murdo
Kay	George	1674	1693	From Alves, appointed as Schoolmaster, Session Clerk, Precentor and Collector. Later rejected in post, but subsequently reinstated. Dismissed from post in 1693
Man	Isobel	1674		In Earlsmill, in fornication with David Brodie
McLalen	George	1674		In fornication with Christian Torrie
Mill	Margaret	1674		In Kintessack, given 9/0d aid by KS
Milne	Elspet	1674		In Kintessack, given 10/0d aid by KS
Murdo	John	1674		In fornication with Elspet Hardie
Phimister	Isobell	1674	1682	In Moy, a habitual curser and swearer, in fornication with John Leal and John MacPherson
Rose	William	1674	1675	Kirk Treasurer and Collector of Penalties, deposed in 1675
Smith	David	1674	1675	Antenuptual fornication with Margaret Clunas
Torrie	Christian	1674		In fornication with George McLalen
Tulloch	Elizabeth	1674		Wife of William Falconer jnr, the Minister of Dyke
Wright	Anna	1674		In Newtown of Grange, given 10/0d aid by Kirk Session

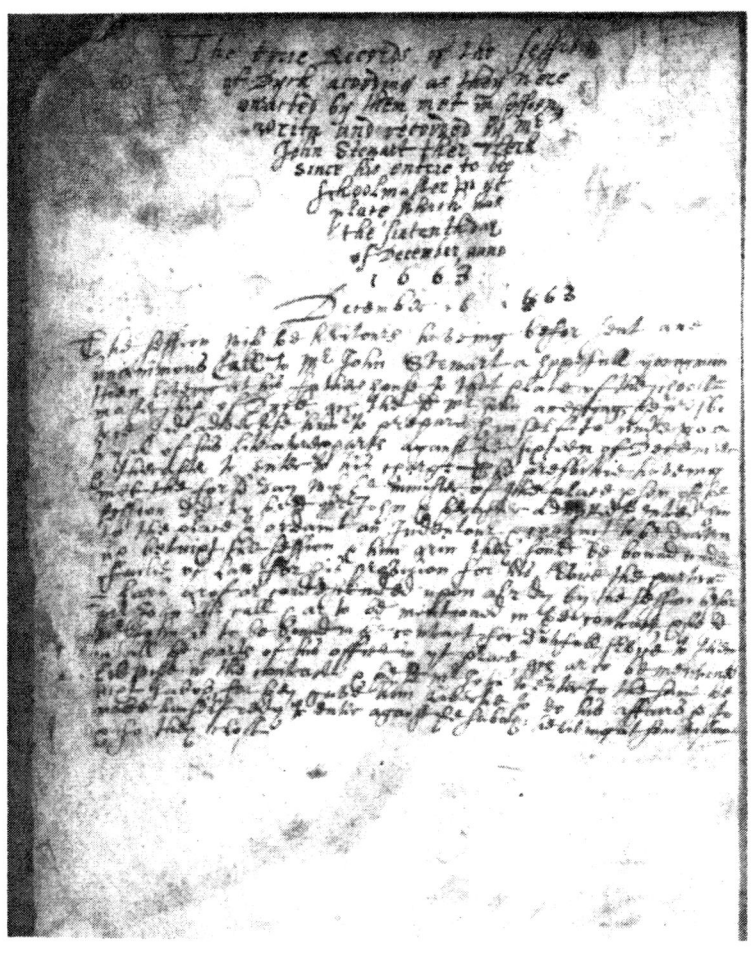

Earliest surviving page of Dyke and Moy Kirk Session Minutes, 1663
in which Mr John Stewart "a hopefull young man" is called as Schoolmaster,
National Archives of Scotland CH2/779/1/5

Poor List of 1665
National Archives of Scotland CH2/779/1/25

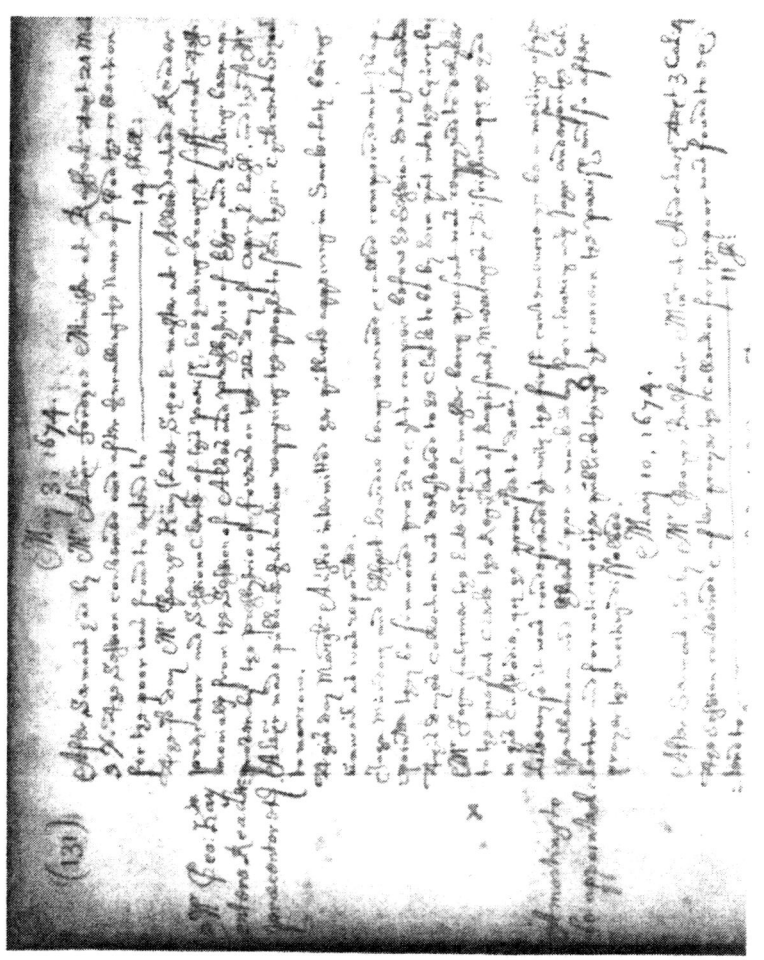

Installation of George Kay as Schoolmaster and Precentor 31st May 1674
National Archives of Scotland CH2/779/1/132

Chapter 3

The Parish of Dyke and Moy from 1675 to 1699

In 1675 the kirk continued to announce new acts, the first of which *"ordained the Kirk Elders to search for drinkers during the tyme of sermon"*. There were also acts anent penny brydalls, and one to discourage masters from making their servants work on the Lord's Day. The Salmon Fishers on the Findhorn were also instructed not to work on the Sabbath. The heritors of the parish designated a plot of land for the building of the new manse as obviously the old one was beyond repair. David Imbrie in Moy was given aid by the Kirk Session to pay for a doctor *"for curing his child of the gravel"*. Janet Lie relapsed into adultery with John Baxter, servant to the Earl of Moray, and Katherin Anderson and Christian Rob were censured for scolding and cursing.

In the same year Mr George Kay, the Schoolmaster, Session Clerk and Precenter was also now chosen as Collector for the parish, and William Rose, the Kirk Treasurer, was discharged from his duties. Later it was noted that the schoolmaster was so busy that he was to be given *"a diligent assistant"*. Lord Braco gave a donation of £34/10/0d Scots money to the Kirk Session for the benefit of the poor of the parish. New Elders were appointed to the Kirk, these being James Cuming for Darnway, Alexander Campbell for Grangegrein, David Duncan for Carsbanks and John Marnoch for Findornhill. Further repairs were made to the thack of the kirk roof, and the cost of pledges for marriage contracts was set as £2 Scots.

On 27th February 1676 the Laird of Brodie recorded in his diary that John Brodie, on of his tenants, had died that day, his wife and three children all having died a few days previously. In November he also records that there were now "Highland Men" in the parish, and also that Conventicles were being held in the area, both in houses and out of doors.[28] In the writings of the Laird of Brodie at this time there is evidence that there was a Chapel or Church at Penick, in the far west of the parish. This may have been related to the Castle of Penick, but there are no other documentary sources which relate to this.

In the same year, on 27th February, the Synod passed an *"Act for the Suppression of Penny Brydels"*, which declared that limited numbers were to be allowed to attend weddings, *"that all pyping fiddling and dancing without doors be discouraged (discouraged)"*, and that *"all obscene, lavicious and promiscuous dancing be in like manner discharged"*. In addition the fee of 2 dollars was to be deposited by the couple – as had been declared locally the previous year. At the same time there was an *"Act anent lykewakes"* which declared that *"... in lyke manner all pyping, fiddling, dancing, sporting, guising and singing be prohibited, and gravitie and sobrietie should be be affected"*. Delinquents were obliged to provide pledges for their penalties.

An act was passed in favour of the school, and plans were designed for the building of a school house for the parish. The lack of a good bridge over the burn was deplored, especially at times of spate, and on 12th November it was *"condescended that some of*

---

[28] National Archives of Scotland. The Diary of Brodie of Brodie. T111.330

the trees in the Churchyard be cutted for that, and agreement with the workmen to build it". The workmen who were to build this bridge across the Muckle Burn at Dyke were identified as John Geddes in Moy, William Tolmie in Dyke and John Lie in Easterbin, all wrights. It seems however, that the eventual erection of a permanent bridge was not to take place for almost another twenty years.

In 1678 Alexander Blackie and John Blackie, "*being in drink*" gave each other a blow on the Lord's Day and were rebuked by the Kirk Session.

1679 saw troubled times in the parish of Dyke and Moy, which led the Laird of Brodie to question "*Quhair ar we?*", but his question seems to have gone unanswered. On 19th June "*The Militia Foot of this place was put out and three horsemen to Stirling*". Soon after this the Militia of the parish was taken away by the Laird of Duffus (probably Gordonstoun) to fight at the Battle of Bothwell Bridge. On 14th August the Laird records that "*Young Gordonstoun cam heir. He said ther was appeiranc of an indulgence to Papists and all others. Lord! Avert!*" [29] An act was passed "*anent staying from the church in tyme of sermon*", but over the next few years the number of breaches of the Sabbath were to increase.

Alexander Brodie, Laird of Brodie, died sometime between midnight and 2 a.m. on Sunday 17th April 1680, and was buried on the 5th of May. Following his death the diaries do not seem to have been continued in the same detail by his son. On 3rd June there was a rendezvous of Militia, this probably referring to the wappinschaw at Kilboyack or a similar event, but just two days later the disputes between Cowbin [Culbin] and Brodie came to a head. By the 17th of June Culbin had men in arms ready to attack Brodie, and there were various meetings to solve the dispute, which seems to have originated, as so many of these local arguments did, over the rights to the peats. At the end of August a further meeting was held at Greishop, but to no effect and the arguments continued. On 12th November there was a "*Setting off and parting of the leases of the Mains of Brodie amongst the tenants*".[30]

On 14th February 1681 Mr George Kay, although currently in the post, was rejected as schoolmaster for the parish due to his "*weaknesses*". This rejection seems to have caused him much dispute with his wife[31], and he eventually seems to have been allowed to continue in the post.

The food shortages of 1682 moved the new Laird of Brodie to write, on 13th September, that "*the crop does threaten want and straits to poor people*". Only a month later he comments "*I heard of many going to Carolina, Pensylvania and New Gersey, I did not relish it*".[32] Obviously the ever-increasing food shortages, which were to become worse over the following two decades, had driven many people to emigrate from rural Morayshire in search of a better life in the Colonies. Thomas Nicol in Grange profaned the Lords Day by "*being wickedly employed in shearing ane horse*", for which he was rebuked.

---

[29] National Archives of Scotland. The Diary of Brodie of Brodie. T111.330
[30] ibid
[31] ibid
[32] ibid

The diaries now begin to give less and less information, but in 1684 they record great falls of snow during October, and the following year a "*great appearance of trouble over the country*".[33] On 15th June 1684 repairs were made to the Kirk Bridge across the Muckle Burn, which must have been the old bridge, and in both August and October the Kirk Elders were "*exhorted to be diligent in observing and faithful in delating*", obviously the loss of penalties from the delinquents was affecting the church funds. This was repeated again in 1687.

In November 1687 an act was again made that "*none shall employ servants without sufficient testimonials*". This was because of the number of 'highlanders' now seeking employment as servants throughout the lowlands of Moray.

William Falconer junior, the Minister, was removed from office in late 1689 or early in 1690, this being recorded in a minute which deprived him, and other ministers under an act which was regarded by many to be "*an unjust eviction of Episcopalian incumbents*".[34] After this there followed a period of three years during which Dyke and Moy did not have a minister. It was during this time that the Rights of Patronage were temporarily abolished, to be restored some 36 years later. In 1691 a request was made for a repetition of a fine imposed on Brodie of Lethen in 1683 for church irregularities, and information on this was supplied to the family of Tulloch at Tannachie in the parish of Forres.[35] On 14th February 1692 Alexander Forbes was admitted to the parish as the new minister. He was the husband of Margaret Stewart.[36]

In March 1693 the schoolmaster's time finally ran out, and George Kay was dismissed. Alexander Findlay, one of the Kirk Elders, officiated as interim Session Clerk, and also as schoolmaster. George Kay promised to amend his ways if re-appointed as schoolmaster, but in view of his past record the Kirk Session decided to advertise for another schoolmaster. Initially Mr Mitchell, the schoolmaster at the Kirk of Glass was considered for the post, but he received a better offer from Turrif. On 22nd June James Murray, the schoolmaster at Kinloss, having precented at the kirk of Dyke just four days earlier, was voted as the new Schoolmaster and Session Clerk.

At the same time the heritors of the parish, the Laird of Brodie and the Laird of Grangehill, together with James Chrystie the Chamberlain to the Earl of Murray, and two of the Kirk Elders, Alexander Findlater and Colin Dunbar, all met to consider the building of a new manse, and a new chamber for the schoolmaster. Also discussed again, after an interval of seventeen years was the building of a new bridge across the burn. "*A bridge to be set upon the Muckle Burn both for the more safer passage for the Scholars to school and for oy^{rs} to the Church, which was frequently hindered because of ye not being a bridge ^{yr}upon*". It was again agreed that trees from the churchyard should be used for this bridge, and the congregation contributed £6/10/8d for the work. James Anderson, the Kirk Treasurer, was appointed to buy a new sackcloth and mortcloth.

Domestic disputes were just as common then as now. Andrew Purse complained to the Kirk Session about Katharin Speediman, his wife, "*her not suffering him to dwell*

---

[33] ibid
[34] National Archives of Scotland GD26/10/48
[35] National Archives of Scotland GD26/10/64
[36] Fasti Ecclesiae Scoticanae

with her and if she might be ordainit to accept of him as her lawful husband and he be allowed to cohabit with her in peace". The judgement of the Kirk Session does not seem to have been recorded.

In 1694 there was a great deal of rebuilding and re-roofing work carried out on the church, and the decision was taken to build kirkyard dykes. The new bridge across the burn, which now seems to have been completed, was found to have been built in a dangerous place, and plans were made to move it "*that people might pass with less hazard*". The work on the kirk continued into 1695, by which time the slaters were able to begin work on the roof. Acts were passed against the sale of drink, especially on the Sabbath, and also against "uncleanness". John Young in Moy "*had purpose of marriage with Margaret Bluntach, she being under scandal of fornication with Colin Dunbar*", the marriage was not permitted until she had undergone censure and purged herself.

"*In the autumn of 1694 and the spring of 1695 Morayshire was visited with a terrible calamity. The coast of the Firth had long been covered with sand, which the currents of the tides carried westwards and threw up into large hills between Nairn and Forres, where it got perfectly dry. Public attention had not been much attracted to that process of nature; but the high winds of these and subsequent years forced the sands eastwards, and dissipated it over the rich Barony of Culbin to its almost total destruction. The River Findhorn was choked up and forced into a new channel. The sand crossed that river and blew eastwards to Burghead, Roseisle, Inverugie and Stotfield, crossed the River Lossie and desolated the country half way to Garmouth.*"[37]

The heritors, comprised of Brodie, Grangehill, Cubin, Moy and the Earl of Moray's Chamberlain met in 1697 to consider the increase "*in the maintenance of the schoolmaster*" and also the building of a new manse for the minister. These were agreed in March 1697 with the costs to be divided amongst the heritors. The old manse was declared to be "*ruinous and in hazard of being quite broken*". The following year, despite the incentives of the increase in his pay, the schoolmaster James Murray decided to go south to further his studies, and was given the six months balance of his salary, which amounted to £14 Scots. James Anderson stood in as Schoolmaster and Session Clerk until the place was filled. Robert Dunbar in Moy and Alexander Findlay were also identified as elders.

The final destruction of the Barony of Culbin during the later years of the 17th century is well documented, and the reader interested in this specific part of the parish can find more detail in 'Moray, Province and People'.[38]

Some of the inhabitants of Dyke and Moy from 1675 to 1699

Anderson	Katherine	1675	Censured for cursing and scolding
Campbell	Alexander	1675	In Grangegreen, Kirk Elder
Clark	Margaret	1675	In Darnaway, in fornication with James Cumming

---

[37] Young. The History of the Parish of Spynie.
[38] Sellar W D H (Ed). Moray, Province and People, p187. 'The Culbin Sands – A Mystery Unravelled", chapter by Sinclair Ross

Clark	Margaret	1675		In Dyke, 18th April 1675 "she is depairted this lyfe"
Cumming	James	1675	1690	In Darnaway, servant to the Earl of Moray and Kirk Elder, in fornication with Margaret Clark. Testament dated 1690
Duncan	David	1675		In Carsebanks, Kirk Elder
Falconer	John	1675		In Carsebanks, cautioner for Margaret Henrie
Hay	John	1675	1677	In Moy, son to Jean Tolmie, censured for unnatural carriage and for fornication with Bessie Smith and Christian Chrystie
Henrie	Margaret	1675		In Carsebanks, in fornication with David Ross
Imbrie	David	1675		In Moy, given aid to pay for a doctor for his child
Marnoch	John	1675		In Findornhill, Kirk Elder
Murray	Jannet	1675		In Muiryhall, censured for cursing
Nicol	Robert	1675	1678	In Moy, in fornication with Janet Dunbar and with Katherin Ker
Rob	Christian	1675		Censured for cursing and scolding
Robertson	Elspet	1675		Given 8/0d aid by Kirk Session
Ross	David	1675		In Carsebanks, in fornication with Margaret Henrie
Smith	Bessie	1675		Servant to James Geddes in Moy, in fornication with John Hay
Sutherland	Marjory	1675		In Grangegreen, profaned Lord's Day
Allan	Bessie	1676		Censured for cursing
Alshioner	Margaret	1676		In Darnaway, aged and sick, given 6/0d aid by Kirk Session
Bell	Margaret	1676		In Grangegreen, profaned Lord's Day
Brodie	John	1676		Tenant in Brodie, died 27th February 1676, his wife and 3 children having died a few days earlier
Clerk	Isobell	1676		In Blackhill, a poor widow given 10/0d aid by Kirk Session
Cowie	James	1676		In Darnaway, profaned Lord's Day
Dowens	Isobell	1676		In Kintessack, diseased, given 6/0d aid
Fraser	John	1676		In Fedden, "sick unto death", given 10/0d aid by Kirk Session
Hay	David	1676		In Grangegreen, husband of Jean Tolmie, profaned Lord's Day
Kinnaird	Thomas	1676		Of Cowbin (Culbin), gave bond to KS
Lie	Alexander	1676		In Easterbin, "an Epilecticle boy", given 5/0d aid by Kirk Session
Lie	John	1676		In Easterbin, Wright, employed to build new bridge
Mitchell	John	1676		Profaned Lord's Day
Smith	James	1676		In Grangegreen, profaned Lord's Day
Tolmie	Jean	1676		Wife of David Hay in Grangegreen

Surname	Forename	Year	Year	Description
Tolmie	William	1676	1685	Wright in Dyke, employed to build new bridge and to repairs seats in kirk lofts
Wright	John	1676		Profaned Lord's Day
Alves	William	1677		In fornication with Margaret Bain
Bain	Margaret	1677		In fornication with William Alves
Bower	William	1677		In Tearie, aged and diseased, given 12/0d aid by Kirk Session
Chrystie	Christian	1677	1680	In Moy, in fornication with John Hay and Thomas Urquhart
Clark	Christian	1677		In Earlsmill, in fornication with Hew MacRottar
Couper	John	1677	1678	In Culbin, diseased, given 6/0d aid by Kirk Session, died in 1678
Dick	Agnes	1677	1678	In Kintessack, sick, given 8/0d aid by KS
Dunbar	John	1677		In Culbin, fornication with Isobell Pyper
James	Bessie	1677		In Lake, bedfast, given 6/8d aid by KS
Ker	James	1677		A 'lame souldier' in Dyke, given 12/0d aid by Kirk Session
Laird	Robert	1677		In fornication with Christian Murdoch
Leal	Alexander	1677		In Moy, aged and sick, given 12/0d aid
MacPherson	John	1677		In Culbin, in fornication with Issobell Phimister
MacRottar	Hew	1677		In Earlsmill, in fornication with Christian Clark
Mill	David	1677		A blind man in Easterbin, given 10/0d aid by Kirk Session
Mill	Hew	1677		In fornication with Katherine Roy
Murdoch	Christian	1677		In fornication with Robert Laird
Pyper	Isobell	1677		In Culbin, fornication with John Dunbar
Roy	Katherine	1677		In Blackhill, fornication with Hew Mill
Smith	James	1677		In Easterbin, aged and sick, given 12/0d aid by Kirk Session
Stevin	Alexander	1677		In Whitemyres, cursing and swearing
Strachan	Isobell	1677		Bedfast, given 4/0d aid by Kirk Session
Tailzeour	Isobell	1677		In fornication with George Young
Young	George	1677		In fornication with Isobell Tailzeour
Blackie	Alexander	1678		Drunk, traded blows with John Blackie
Blackie	John	1678		Drunk, traded blows with Alexr Blackie
Clunas	John	1678		In fornication with Jean Kinnaird
Fraser	John	1678		A blind man in Wellhill, given 6/0d aid
Ker	Katherine	1678		In Moy, in fornication with Robert Nicol
Kinnaird	Isobell	1678		In Darklass, sick, granted 6/0d aid by KS
Kinnaird	Jean	1678		In fornication with John Clunas
Kyle	Elspet	1678	1679	In fornication with James Tailzeour
Sutherland	Agnes	1678		Bedfast, given 4/0d aid by Kirk Session
Tailzeour	James	1678		In fornication with Elspet Kyle
Thomson	Janet	1678	1679	In Kintessack, in fornication with William Brodie, W.S. in Edinburgh
Bremner	Thomas	1679		In fornication with Agnes Hay
Eadie	Christian	1679		Profand Lord's Day

Forsyth	Marjorie	1679		In Grangegreen, cursed James Hardie
Hardie	James	1679	1680	In Grangegreen, cursed by Marjorie Forsyth and in fornication with Elspet Mill in 1680
Hay	Agnes	1679		In fornication with Thomas Bremner
Badon	Robert	1680		In Grangegreen, in fornication with Elspet Cant
Brodie	Alexander	1680		Brodie of Brodie, Laird of Brodie, died Sunday 17th April 1680
Cant	Elspet	1680		In Grangegreen, in fornication with Robert Badon
Mill	Elspet	1680		In Grangegreen, in fornication with James Hardie
Peterkin	Margaret	1680		In Kintessack, in fornication with William Watson
Urquhart	Thomas	1680		In fornication with Christian Chrystie
Watson	William	1680		In Kintessack, in fornication with Margaret Peterkin
Dowglas	Mungo	1681		In Darnaway, in fornication with Katherin Dunbar
Dunbar	Katherin	1681		In Darnaway, in fornication with Mungo Dowglas
Bell	James	1682		In Darnaway, fornication with Jean Innes
Fordyce	James	1682		In fornication with Margaret Mill
Innes	Jean	1682		In Darnaway, in fornication with James Bell
Mill	Alexander	1682		In Culbin, in fornication with Janet Smith in Kintessack
Mill	David	1682		In Culbin, in fornication with Jean Mill
Mill	Jean	1682		In Culbin, in fornication with David Mill
Mill	Margaret	1682		In fornication with James Fordyce
Nicol	Thomas	1682		In Grangegreen, profaned Lord's Day by shearing a horse
Pyper	James	1682		In Muirtown, in fornication with Janet Smith in Grange
Smith	Janet	1682		In Kintessack, in fornication with Alexander Mill in Culbin
Smith	Janet	1682		In Grangegreen, in fornication with James Pyper in Muirtown
Couper	Christian	1683		In Grangegreen, in fornication with William Frisk
Cumming	James	1683		In Tearie, in fornication with Elspet Strachan
Frisk	William	1683		In Grangegreen, in fornication with Christian Couper
Petrie	John	1683		In Earnhill, in fornication with Margaret Stewart in Delpottie
Stewart	Margaret	1683		In Delpottie, fornication with John Petrie
Strachan	Elspet	1683		In Tearie, in fornication with James Cumming

Cunninghame	Bessie	1684		In fornication with John Ross
Ross	John	1684		In fornication with Bessie Cunnunghame
Tolmie	Elspet	1684		In Grangegreen, in fornication with Alexander Vass
Vass	Alexander	1684		In fornication with Elspet Tolmie
Anderson	Lillias	1685		In Wellhill, in fornication with Robert Dunbar in Leyhill
Cloggie	Agnes	1685		In Sandiscote, in fornication with Alexander Lauson
Cumming	David	1685		In Tearie, his testament dated 1685
Cumming	Robert	1685		In Tearie, in fornication with Helen Kinnaird in Culbin
Dunbar	Robert	1685		In Leyhill, in fornication with Lillias Anderson
Heriwood	John	1685		In Tearie, drunk on the Lord's Day
Kinnaird	Helen	1685		In Culbin, in fornication with Robert Cumming in Tearie
Lauson	Alexander	1685		In Kintessack, in fornication with Agnes Cloggie
Lyon	Agnes	1685		In Moy, fornication with Patrick Watson
Monro	Elspet	1685		In Darnaway, in fornication with John Shearer in Earlsmill
Petrie	Isobell	1685		In Fedden, assaulted by her sister Jean
Petrie	Jean	1685		In Fedden, struck her sister Isobell on Sabbath
Shearer	John	1685		In Earlsmill, in fornication with Elspet Monro at Darnaway
Watson	Patrick	1685		In Kintessack, in fornication with Agnes Lyon in Moy
Dunbar	James	1686		In fornication with Lillias Urquhart
Gowans	Jannet	1686		In fornication with John Laird
Laird	John	1686		In fornication with Jannet Gowans
Urquhart	Lillias	1686		In fornication with James Dunbar
Fraser	Alexander	1687		In Darnaway, in fornication with Jannet Watson
Watson	Jannet	1687		In fornication with Alexander Fraser
Bremner	William	1688		In fornication with Christian Laing
Grant	John	1688		Of Moyness, his testament dated 1688
Hay	Bessie	1688		In fornication with James Williamson
Laing	Christian	1688		In fornication with William Bremner
Paterson	Jean	1688		In Darnaway, in fornication with Richard Pixtoun
Pixtoun	Richard	1688		In Darnaway, in fornication with Jean Paterson
Williamson	James	1688	1689	In Fedden, profaned Lord's Day, also in fornication with Bessie Hay
Dowglas	James	1689		In Darnaway, in fornication with Isobell Turk
Turk	Isobell	1689		In fornication with James Dowglas
Forbes	Alexander	1692	1708	Minister at Dyke

Surname	Forename	Year	Year2	Description
Stewart	Margaret	1692		Wife of Alexander Forbes, Minister
Allan	Christian	1693		Wife of Nicol Reat in Boat of Findhorn, made "reproachable speeches"
Alves	James	1693	1694	In fornication with Agnes Walker
Anderson	James	1693		Kirk Treasurer
Davidson	David	1693	1727	In Whitemyres, given aid by KS in 1727
Davidson	Lachlan	1693		In adultery with Betrix Moir
Dunbar	Colin	1693		Kirk Elder
Findlater	Alexander	1693	1695	Kirk Elder, Treasurer, acted as Session Clerk and Schoolmaster during vacancies
Fisher	Jean	1693		In fornication with Alexander Milne
Gilbert	John	1693	1694	In Earlsmill, in fornication with Janet McInteer
Grant	John	1693		In Wellheads, husband of Margaret Tulloch
McInteer	Janet	1693	1694	In Earlsmill, in fornication with John Gilbert
Milne	Alexander	1693		In fornication with Jean Fisher
Milne	David	1693		In Boat of Findhorn, made complaint against Christian Allan
Moir	Beatrix	1693		In adultery with Lachlan Davidson
Murray	James	1693		From Kinloss, appointed Schoolmaster, Session Clerk and Precenter on 22nd June 1693
Peterkin	James	1693	1694	In Logiebuchany, in fornication with Isabel Shearer and with Isobell Baxter
Purse	Alexander	1693		His wife Katherine Speediman would not let him live with her
Reat	Nicol	1693		In Boat of Findhorn
Shearer	Isabel	1693		In Logiebuchany, in fornication with James Peterkin
Simpson	Margaret	1693		Censured, stood in sackcloth for adultery
Speediman	Katherine	1693		Wife to Alexander Purse, but would not let him live with her
Tulloch	Margaret	1693		Wife of John Grant in Wellheads, her testament dated 1693
Turnbull	Alexander	1693		In Darnaway, in fornication with Janet Willands
Walker	Agnes	1693	1694	In fornication with James Alves
Willands	Janet	1693	1694	Servant to David Davidson in Darnaway, in fornication with Alexander Turnbull
Anderson	Bessie	1694		Daughter to John Anderson in Moy, in fornication with James Anderson
Anderson	James	1694		In Moy, in fornication with Bessie Anderson
Anderson	John	1694		In Moy, father to Bessie Anderson
Baxter	Isobell	1694		In fornication with James Peterkin
Blackie	Isobell	1694		In Grangegreen, in fornication with William Keith
Dunbar	Robert	1694		In Moy, stood surety for Wm Urquhart

Falconer	Isabel	1694	Daughter to William Falconer in Kincorth, received aid from Kirk Session
Falconer	William	1694	In Kincorth, father to Isabel Falconer
Keith	William	1694	In Grangegreen, in fornication with Isobell Blackie
Milne	Jean	1694	In fornication with Peter Thomson
Murdoch	Bessie	1694	Given £2 by Kirk Session to pay for her husbands funeral
Thomson	Peter	1694	In fornication with Jean Milne
Urquhart	William	1694	Servant to the Laird of Grangehill
Badon	John	1695	In fornication with Emelia Gaa
Clark	James	1695	In Blackhill, in fornication with Janet Gowens
Gaa	Emilia	1695	In fornication with John Badon
Gowens	Janet	1695	In Blackhill, in fornication with James Clark
Gowie	William	1695	Kirk Officer, given £1/6/8d to buy shoes
Smith	Gilbert	1695	In Carselands, censured for fighting on Sabbath

Poor List 1675
National Archives of Scotland CH2/779/1/150

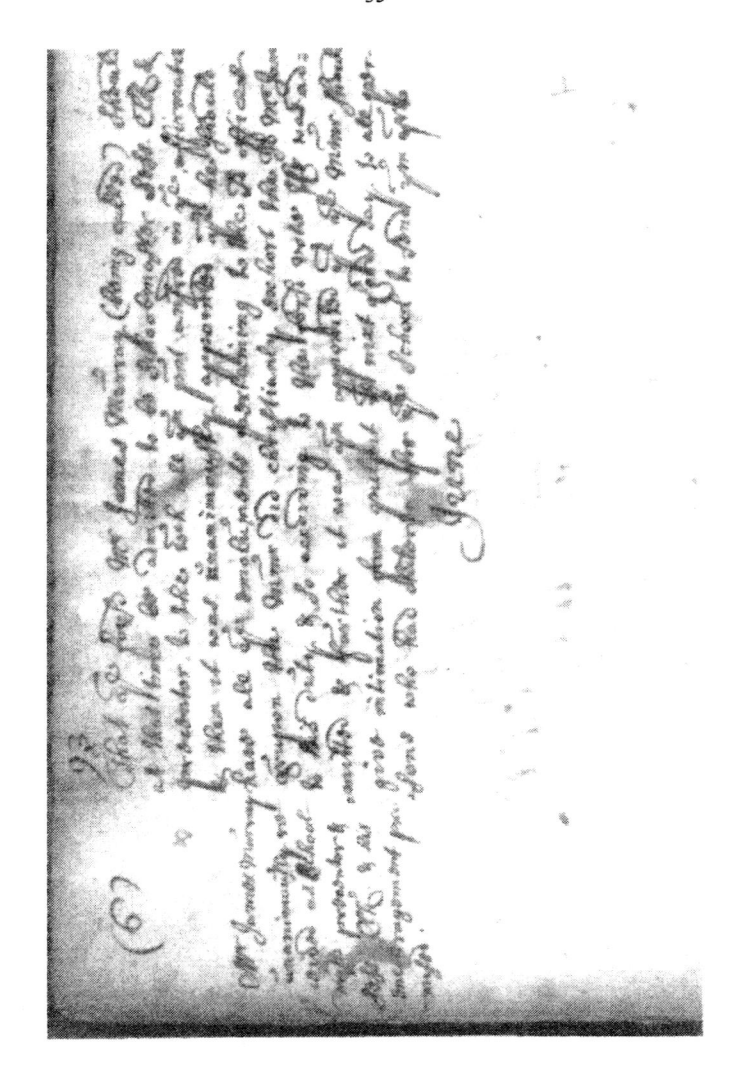

Installation of James Murray as Schoolmaster and Session Clerk 22nd June 1693
National Archives of Scotland CH2/779/2/7

The true Records
of the Session of Dyke according
as they were enacted Sessional-
lie by the members thereof
written & recorded be-
Mr James Murray their
Clk since his entrie to
be School-master in y[e]
place which was y[e]
twentie second day
of June anno
1693

June 26.

The s[ai]d day collected for y[e] poor 0. 16. 6
The s[ai]d day according to y[e] appointment of y[e]
last Sess: the ministr [...] advised from [...]
y[ere] was a Schoolmaster [...]
that such as had Children [...] to school.

July 2.

The s[ai]d day [...] collected — 1. 09. 10
The s[ai]d day [...] upon a supplicat[ion] from y[e]
parioch of [...] presenting a [...]
[...] — 11. 00. 00
The s[ai]d day after Sermon y[e] Sess: considered y[e] [...]
[...]

Page from Kirk Session Minutes 25[th] June 1693
National Archives of Scotland CH2/779/2/7

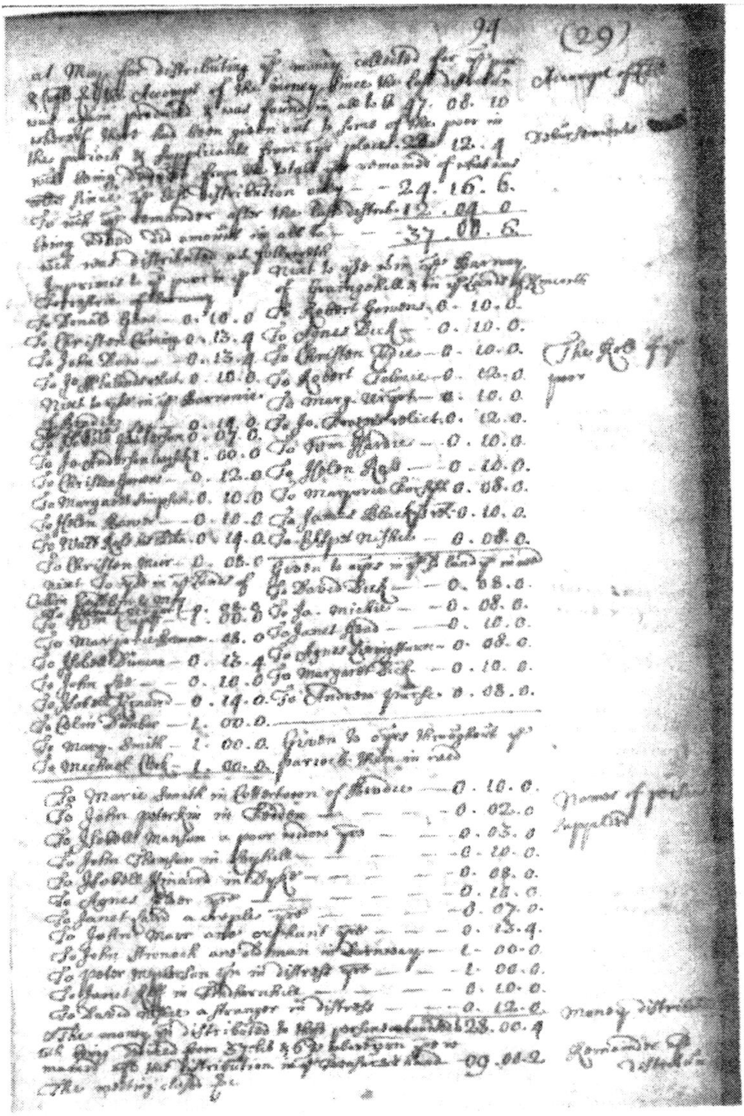

Poor List 1694
National Archives of Scotland CH2/779/2/29

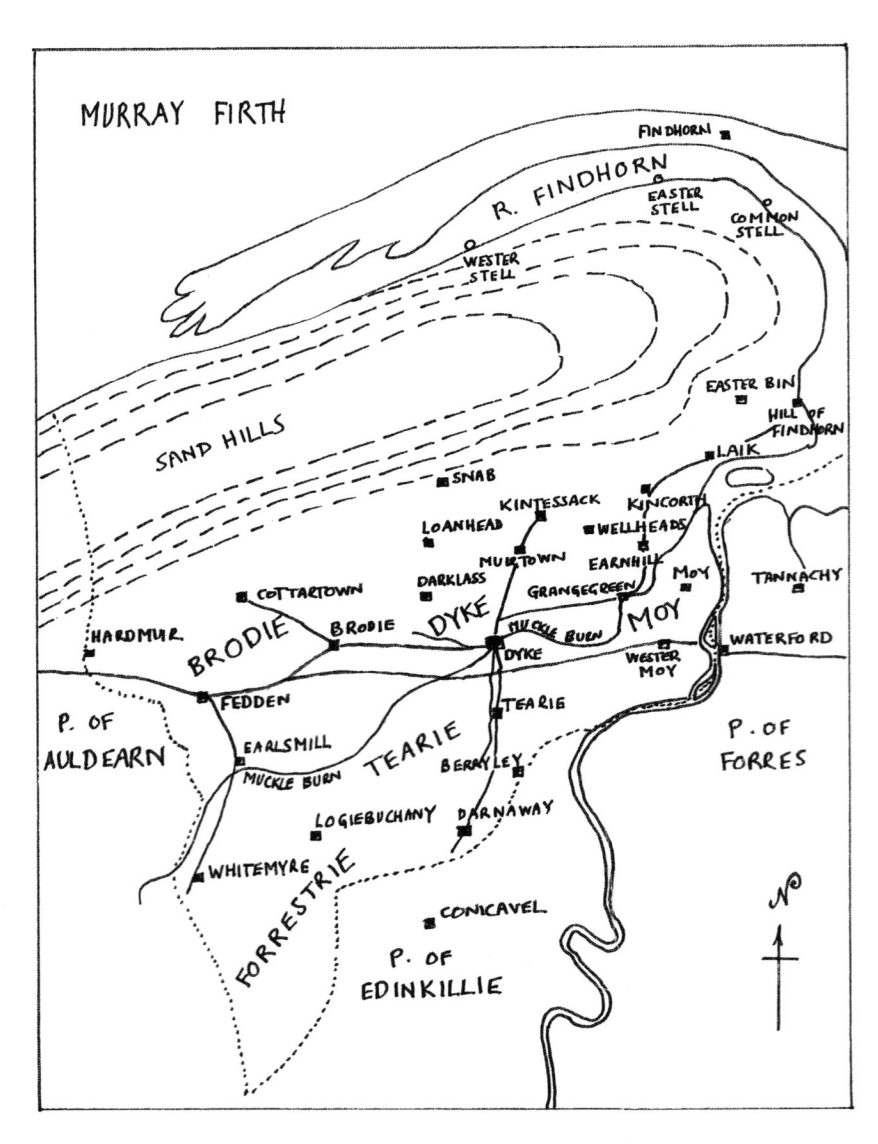

Sketch map of the Parish of Dyke and Moy ca 1700

Chapter 4

The Parish of Dyke and Moy from 1700 to 1724

In 1700 the Laird of Grangehill provided land for the building of a new schoolhouse with a chamber for the schoolmaster, and early in 1701 Mr Alexander Tod was appointed Schoolmaster and Session Clerk. At last the handwriting in the Session Minutes becomes more legible. The Session complained that the rents of the Chapel Croft, which had been mortified by William Falconer many years previously for the benefit of the poor, had not been received during all the time his son had been in possession of it, and action was commenced to recover these losses to the Poor's Fund.

The way of life by the early 18th century had changed little over the past hundred years. The landowners had their castles or mansion houses and the main tenant farmers had their houses in the fermtouns, these now sometimes having four rooms, glass in the windows rather than board shutters, and maybe a roof of slate rather than the thatch of earlier times. For the subtenants and cottagers, however, the thatched but-and-ben was still the main dwelling, although some now had outbuildings to house the beasts. The runrig way of agriculture continued, and formed little more than subsistence farming. Communications were poor, the main Kings Highway through the parish was the best-maintained route, but even this was little more than a dirt track prone to flooding in the winter. The local tracks between the settlements meandered among the runrig strips, and the traveller needed to find the best route depending on his mode of transport and the weather.

The destruction of the old village of Findhorn, across the water from Culbin, took place in 1701 (some sources suggest 1702), probably during the autumn, and was caused by a severe storm from the NE associated with very high tides, which breached the sandbar on which the old village was built. This event changed the nature of the mouth of the river, and destroyed the fishings both at Culbin and Findhorn.

In 1702 the "*whole of the Lands, Barony and Estate of Culbin*" and other lands belonging to Colonel Hugh Grant of Moy, were listed as "*That part called Mains of Culbin, Hill of Findhorn, the boat upon the Water of Findhorn, and the muscle and salmond fishings, Machrodder alias Mirrietown, Aikenhead alias Rauchkane, Binn or Middle Binn, Laich or Sandiepied, Deleith, also known as Dalpottie, with the Mill of Dalpottie, and the Chappell of St Ninian except for the manse. Also listed were Earnhill, Easter Binn, Frierscroft also know as Kintessack, the Miln of Moy and Moy Croft, Grangehill, Buichtillies with the boat, Grangegreen, Muirtoun and the Churchlands of Moy. These lands were bounded by The Green Meiring which divides the lands of Washing Stones and the said Churchlands in the east and the lands of Bankhead on the north part. The Greengate which leads from Moy to the Water of Findhorn in the south, and the Common Road from the Toun of Moy to the Port of Findhorn in the west. The lands of Moy, commonly called Wester Moy, comprehends*

Moy, Moycairn, Croftmalloch and Kirklands of Moy".[39] During the early 18th century the lands of Drumreach, Lake and even some parts of Binsness '*have been covered*'.[40]

The Earl of Moray donated 250 merks left by his father for the use of the poor of the parish, with 50 merks to be distributed immediately and the remainder to be added to the Poor's Fund. The monies were placed in the hands of Alexander Findlater, the Kirk Treasurer. The Minister and the Earl of Moray held further discussion about the building of the new school and also of a Church Yard, presumably this meant the church yard dykes. The Laird of Grangehill agreed with the 'measons' regarding the building of the new 'Grammar School', but the building of the school was delayed by Grangehills tardiness. A further act was passed anent penny weddings, with '*promiscuous dancing*' to be banned at all weddings.

Also in 1702 John Anderson, a native of the parish but later a Writer to the Signet in Edinburgh, had left the sum of 2000 merks to provide a salary for a "*Mistris for Education of the female sex*", providing the Laird of Brodie should grant right for a schoolhouse. Janet Chalmers, "*a Gentlewoman of Good Repute presently at Skibo in Sutherland*", was chosen for the post and given a year's trial, being admitted on 2nd June, with testimonials. The building of the Grammar School was commenced on the same day. The Kirk Session may have been fearful of the fact that a Popish schoolmistress could at some future time be appointed, and they inserted the following clause in the minutes; "*If as the Lord forbid in after ages Popery should prevail in the said parioch and a Popish school mistris offered to be settled then and immediately the thereafter the school shall break up – and the inducements shall fall and pertain to the poor of the parioch ...*".

In 1705 Archibald Dunbar, squarewright in Graingegrein, agreed to build a new loft in the east end of the church of Dyke for the sum of £120 Scots. Considerting the paucity of Elders, the Session nominate for election
    Alexander Dunbar of Moy (not elected)
    John Dunbar of Kirkhill (not elected)
    William Dunbar in Wellhead in Wester Moy (elected)
    Archibald Dunbar, squarewright in Graingegrein (elected)
    William Falconer in Carsbanks (not elected)
    William Bremner in Leyhill (elected)
    Alexander Nicolson, Master of the new school of Dyke (elected)
    John Williamson in Blackhillock, the Earl of Moray's Chamberlain (elected).

The minister, Mr Alexander Forbes, was unwell at this time, and fearing his demise Mr John Cumming was chosen as minister of Dyke. His appointment was not required however, as in 1707 Alexander Forbes was restored to health. His recovery was not sustained, and he died in April 1708

On 23rd May 1708 "*This day Mr John Corbat, probationer, read ane order from the United Presbyteries of Forres and Inverness, appointing him to declare the church vacant. Mr Forbes who had been Minister here having been removed by* death".

---

[39] National Archives of Scotland GD23/9/18
[40] Old Statistical Account for the Parish of Dyke and Moy

On 10th July 1709 the Church pronounced an edict for calling a minister. *"Mr James Chalmers, probationer, was called to be their minister, with which call the Presbytery did concur"*. On 14th September the Presbytery *"... did proceed to ordain Mr James Chalmers and did settle him as Minister of Dyke, with the unanimous consent and approbation of all concerned"*. James Chalmers was minister of Dyke and Moy from 1709 until 1726, at which time he was removed to Aberdeen.[41] A tree in the churchyard was cut and squared to finally provide a bridge over the Muckle Burn.

On 27th November Mr Alexander Philp *"the Session being satisfied with his testimonials and the recommendations of the Presbytery"* was appointed Schoolmaster and Session Clerk, and *"because he cannot sing and is thereby incapacitated to exercise the office of Precentor in the said parish he therefore oblidges himself to provide a sufficient Precentor from time to time to the satisfaction of the parish"*. Penny Weddings were still causing disruption to the sensibilities of the Kirk Session, and on 4th December an Act anent penny weddings was pronounced *"for preventing abuses at both contracts and weddings that the parties contracted shall be obliged to keep neither their contract nor their wedding in ane Ale House, that they shall have no promiscuous dancing and that no more than sixteen persons on both sides shall convene"*. This shows that not only weddings but the contracts, or engagements, were a source of celebration.

The schoolmaster, Mr Tod, after eight years in the post, was removed in September 1709 *"Mr Tod is not only absent but also as it is reported is licensed to preach the Gospel as probationer and consequently uncapable to discharge the duties incumbent as schoolmaster in this place. All present unanimously declare that the school is vacant"*. The following month Alexander Tod gave in his demission as schoolmaster and received a gratuity for his former services. It was also noted that *"Most of the windows of the kirk want glass and wyre. Alexander Nicolson, Kirk Elder and Glasier in Dyke is to fill them up with glass and wyre and that with all possible dispatch seeing the winter approaches"*. He completed the work before the winter and early the next year presented a bill for £64/17/2d to the Session.

In 1710 the idea of building local bridges seems to have caught on, and William Walker desired to cut a tree in the Kirkyard to make a bridge over the Burn of Moy. Permission was granted by the Session, the work to be overseen by Archibald Dunbar. The trees in the Kirkyard of Moy were also all to be felled and sold, and were purchased by Colin Troup.

Elspet Tolmie *"had allowed Colin Leal to come so frequently to her house and at so unseasonable hours after she had been forbidden both by Archibald Dunbar, Kirk Elder, and her own brother"*, that she was required to appear before the Session to explain herself. She answered that they had 'designs on marriage'. David Piterkin, James Young, James Duncan and Alexander Allan were all censured for fishing for salmon in the Water of Findhorn on the Sabbath. They said that they had only drawn their net through the water to spread it on the other side. There were three witnesses against the salmon fishers, these being Alexander Duncan, aged about 50; John Leal aged about 60 and John Forsyth of a similar age, all married men. The Kirk Session

---

[41] Fasti Ecclesiae Scoticanae

felt that the witnesses may have harboured a grudge against the miscreants, and as it was a first offence the fishers were rebuked and dismissed.

By 1711 the number of cases being dealt with before the Kirk Session was increasing rapidly. George Lie in the Hill of Findorn and Peter Sutor in the Lake were censured for being in the house of George Dunbar in Kintessack and drinking during the time of the afternoon sermon. Alexander Taylor in the hill of Findhorn "*took a gun out of William Falconer's house in Carsbanks and went to Peter Sutors house where he offered* (threatened) *to shoot him*". Gilbert Leal in Kintessack was censured for antenuptual fornication, but Anne Dunbar, the midwife, stated that the child was very weak "*and had not completed the ordinary time*", so the Session could not prove that it had been conceived before marriage and the case was dropped. Alexander Sinclair in Moy and Robert Bluntach in Delpottie did drink "*last Lord's Day the whole afternoon in Peter Thomson's house in Dyke*" and it was reported by the Elders to Alexander Findlay, the Ruling Elder, that the Lord's Day was frequently encroached on throughout the parish by brewing late on Saturday night. Anne Dunbar in Kintessack carried ale down to the Hill of Findorn to sell on the Sabbath "*whereby she not only absented herself from church but tempted and ensnared others in that place to do the like*". She confessed and was rebuked. Whether it was the effects of the ale or not, four of James Fordyce's servants, David Sutherland, James Leal, Agnes Ogilvy and Janet Hay were censured at least twice for their unseemly carriage with one another and for swearing in their master's yard. Agnes seemed to have been the ringleader.

New Kirk Elders were elected in 1712, these being Alexander Geddes in Tearie, James Allan at the Miln of Brodie, John Dunbar in Newtown of Grangehill, John Wilson and James Dick in Moy, Peter Couper in Kintessack, William Walker in Earnhill and Robert Gowie in Easterbin. Among their first tasks was to deal with Isabell Callum, who was contracted to marriage with John Smith, but she had been in adultery with a man in Auldearn and was with child, and permission for the marriage was deferred. Alexander Black and his wife Janet Bremner, in Wellhill, were not the happiest of couples, and were censured "*for their unchristian and scandalous behaviour by reason of their frequent beating, scolding and cursing of one another*". The Minister and the Elders went to their house to speak to them. William Paterson was censured for opening a drinking house on the Sabbath.

William Walker was chosen Ruling Elder in 1713. Peter Thomson younger, Peter Baxter, Robert Thomson and Alexander Taylor were censured for fishing on the Sabbath. Two of the men had stayed home to look to their boat, but the other two spent the afternoon in "*following a fowl who kills salmond* [possibly an Osprey], *and they took some salmond from the said fowl and brought it home the same night*". This was one case that the Session could not resolve as one of the witnesses had flown. They also stated that the "*bleeching and drying of cloath on the Lord's Day to be a Breach of Sabbath*", as was the gleaning of pease and the drying of corn.

In the same year "*The Session taking into consideration the custome observed in this place of burying the deid so soon after expiring agreed unanimously that none should be buried except in caice of urgent necessity until forty eighth hours after expiring*". William Findlater, the son of Alexander Findlater in Brodie, was censured for his adultery with Elspet Waxter, and was appointed to appear in sackcloth each Sabbath for a twelve-month. As he never appeared before the Kirk Session he was threatened with excommunication, but eventually both he and Elspet Waxter served their punishment. William Bain in Cars Banks "*last Sabbath in the twighlight came to William Walker's house and gave him and his servants ill language*". Elspet Christie and Janet Peterkin fought over a seat in the kirk; the eventual winner was not recorded but both were censured.

Some new names appear amongst the list of Elders in 1714, these being Alexander Findlater, Alexander Nicolson, William Bremner and Archibald Dunbar. William Findlater and Elspet Waxter did not have to serve their full year in sackcloth, being absolved at the end of July 1714, together with Margaret Laing, who had also spent several Sabbath days standing in sackcloth. Andrew Nicolson was appointed Ruling Elder, and Janet Gilzean, Christian Gowans, Janet Peterkin and Isabell Carrach were all censured for gathering hips and berries on the Sabbath.

In 1715 a tree was felled to make a bridge across the Meikle Burn at Chappel Croft, and William Bremner became Ruling Elder. James Peterkin was described as a "*contumacious adulterer*", and the Poor List continued to increase, there now being 37 people receiving aid from the Kirk. Janet Thomson, the schoolmistress in Findornhill, was given an allowance of £1 quarterly "*so long as she keeps that school*".

Christian Smith took over the position of schoolmistress at Findornhill the following year, and also in 1716 Jean Robertson, a servant of Chamberlain Russell at Earlsmiln "*brought forth a dead child in such a clandestine manner as makes her suspect of infant-murder*". The Kirk Session felt fit to acquaint the Civil Judge with the details and ordered that the child should not be buried "*until desired by the said Sheriff-depute*". She was imprisoned in the meantime, probably in the tollbooth of Forres, but there are no further details of the case. Robert Gowrie in Dyke, sometime tenant in Easterbin, left 100 merks to the Kirk Session for the poor.

James Phimister and James Petrie in Wellhill, John Leal in Kincorth and John Forsyth in Moy, all salmon fishers, were all caught fishing on the Sabbath, but to make matters worse they were also said to be on Edinkillie lands. This was probably in the Darnaway reaches of the Findhorn River, as it was noted at this period that the estate of Darnaway now fell in the parish of Edinkillie. The parish boundary here seems to have been very flexible. David Tolmie, James Cunningham and Robert Dunbar, all living in Dyke, saw the Miln of Grangehill grinding on the Sabbath. James Findlay, the miller, who was employed by Archibald Dunbar, one of the Kirk Elders, blamed it all on his wife Bessie Hay. Both were censured.

In October 1717 Alexander Philp, the Schoolmaster and Session Clerk, demitted office and was granted a gratuity of £12 and given a testimonial from the parish. The following month Mr William Maitland "*a young man well testified*" was given a trial and then appointed as Schoolmaster, Session Clerk and Precenter on 17th November. In 1718 John Alves, the teacher of the Charity School at Kintessack was paid his salary of £9. Isobel McPherson was severely censured for the fornication with James Peterkin, he now being an excommunicat person.

There were additions to the list of Elders in 1719, these included James Brodie of Brodie, Ludovick Dunbar of Moy, Alexander Cumming and Alexander Lee in Whitemyre, David McCulloch in Darnaway, Alexander Lee in Moy and Alexander Maver in Earnhill. The inclusion of the Elders from Darnaway and Whitemyre shows that the comments made some three years earlier suggesting that Darnaway was in the parish of Edinkillie were probably misguided. John Leal and his wife Henret Demster were in Breach of Sabbath when they carried home victuals from the mill in a horse and cart.

In May 1720 Mr William Maitland, the Schoolmaster, Session Clerk and Precentor demitted office. On his leaving the school it was suggested that Mr Alexander Dick, Professor of Humanity, should succeed him, but this led to some disagreement among the heritors. The matter was referred to the Presbytery who judged that *"the most pacifick method* [would be] *to make choice of another rather than Mr Dick, though they judge him in every way sufficient for that office"*. The suggested that Robert Gowie, Student in Philosophie, should serve for the next half year. A later enquiry into the conduct of the Session over the case of the schoolmaster found that some of their number had *"acted a very unsuitable part"* and Alexander Findlater and Alexander Cumming were *"laid aside from their office"*, although the other Elders were allowed to continue. There was a complaint made against Janet Balmano in Darclas by James Smith there and also by Margaret Cunningham in Dyke because of her scandalous and unchristian expressions.

Mr Alexander Turing seems to have been appointed as Schoolmaster sometime after this, and he demitted office on 25th November 1722, to be replaced by James Gordon, the Schoolmaster of Grange. The Session Minutes at this time are very poor.

In 1723 William Findlater was excommunicated for his fornication with Isobel Hay, and William McBeth and Janet Drowton, being unable to produce any evidence of their marriage, were deemed to be cohabiting. The salmon fishers; Alexander Nicolson, George McKay, James Dick, John Dunbar and James and John Young, were all censured for breach of Sabbath, and the last two also for contumacy. A new window was put into the church to provide some light for the Grammar School loft, and William Bower proved to be a totally useless witness when called to testify against Peter Thomson, Isabel Gowans and Margaret Thomson as he had been so drunk that he was unable to remember anything.

In 1724 William Findlater, still excommunicated, was accused of troubling Christian Tolmie, the daughter of Peter Tolmie and Isobel Williamson in Longhill. An excommunicated person at this time, of course, was not allowed to attempt to hold any non-essential conversation with any other person, or to hold any employment. John Milne in Blackhill was censured for employing him, as was John Forsyth in Grangegreen. Kathryn Kemp, a widow in Teary, was also censured for allowing him and his children to help with the shearing.

Girsel Tory and Kathrin Eddie appeared before the Kirk Session accused of *"praying curses"* against David Tolmie. He had heard them call him an *"Egyptian Fanny"* in the house of Elizabeth Duncan. [The word 'Egyptian' at this time usually referred to gypsies]. Both Elizabeth Duncan and Margaret Stewart, a widow, heard this, and said that they had also heard the women make wishes that he (David Tolmie) would not thrive, and that he might die an ill death on the highway. Girsel Tory and Kathrin Eddie were sharply rebuked, but at the same time David Tolmie was advised not to give them any provocation.

Some of the inhabitants of Dyke and Moy from 1700 to 1724

Surname	Forename	Year	Year	Notes
Leitch	William	1702		In Darnaway, his testament dated 1702
Dunbar	Robert	1704		In Grangegreen, testament dated 1704
Barclay	Katherine	1708		Wife of William Dunbar at Mill of Moy, her testament dated 1708
Dunbar	William	1708		At Mill of Moy, husband of Katherine Barclay
Allan	Margaret	1709	1710	In fornication with Thomas Monro
Bremner	William	1709	1729	In Tearie, Kirk Elder, Ruling Elder in 1715, bought seat in south side of Wester Loft of Kirk in 1729
Chalmers	James	1709	1726	Minister at Dyke
Chrystie	Elspet	1709		In fornication with Alexander Hardie
Dunbar	Archibald	1709	1714	Kirk Elder
Dunbar	William	1709		In Wester Moy, Kirk Elder
Findlater	Alexander	1709	1711	Kirk Elder, sometime Ruling Elder
Gowans	Janet	1709		In Moy, in Breach of Sabbath
Hardie	Alexander	1709		In fornication with Elspet Chrystie
Hay	Elspet	1709		In Moy, in Breach of Sabbath
Leal	Colin	1709	1710	In Grangegreen, in scandalous behaviour with Elspet Tolmie
MacMichael	William	1709		In fornication with Christian Smith
Monro	Thomas	1709	1710	In fornication with Margaret Allan
Murdoch	Isobell	1709		In Blackhill, in Breach of Sabbath
Murdoch	Janet	1709		In fornication
Nicolson	Alexander	1709	1752	Glasier in Dyke, Kirk Elder, sometime Ruling Elder, appointed Kirk Treasurer in 1726, died in 1752
Philp	Alexander	1709		Appointed Schoolmaster and Session Clerk 27th November 1709
Smith	Christian	1709	1711	In fornication with William MacMichael
Tolmie	Elspet	1709	1710	In Grangegreen, scandalous behaviour with Colin Leal
Allan	Alexander	1710		In Moy, salmon fisher, fished on Sabbath
Austie	Isabel	1710		In Grangegreen, on Poor List
Bain	Robert	1710		In Grangegreen, aged about 30, witness against Colin Leal
Blackie	Alexander	1710	1714	In Kincorth, father of child by Isobell Hay
Campbell	John	1710		His house burned down, given £3 aid
Chrystie	Christian	1710		In Wellhill, on Poor List
Clerk	Isabel	1710		On Poor List
Davidson	James	1710		On Poor List

Dick	Agnes	1710	1715	In Grangegreen, on Poor List, her funeral cost £1/0/10d in 1715
Dunbar	John	1710	1732	In Grangegreen, a married man, aged about 50 in 1710, witness against Colin Leal. Kirk Elder, Ruling Elder in 1727
Dunbar	Thomas	1710		In Grangegreen, married man aged about 40, witness against Colin Leal
Duncan	Alexander	1710		In Moy, aged about 50, witness against the salmon fishers
Duncan	James	1710		In Moy, salmon fisher, fished on Sabbath
Duncan	Margaret	1710		On Poor List
Edie	Christian	1710		In Grangegreen, on Poor List, given additional 3/0d aid by Kirk Session
Edison	James	1710		On Poor List
Falconer	Christian	1710		In Grangegreen, married woman aged about 40, witness against Colin Leal
Falconer	Margaret	1710		Given 6/0d aid by Kirk Session
Findlay	James	1710		In Grangegreen, married man aged about 50, witness against Colin Leal
Fordyce	James	1710	1713	In Dyke, his servants censured for cursing and swearing on the Sabbath
Forsyth	Colin	1710		In fornication with Janet Gow
Forsyth	John	1710		In Moy, aged about 60, witness against the salmon fishers
Friese	Colin	1710		In Dyke, censured by Kirk Session
Gow	Janet	1710		In fornication with Colin Forsyth
Gowans	Elspet	1710		On Poor List
Gowrie	Alexander	1710		On Poor List
Hay	Alexander	1710		In Grangegreen, married man aged about 40, witness against Colin Leal
Hay	Christian	1710		With child, refused to name father, excommunicated
Hay	Isobell	1710		In Wellhill, in fornication with Alexander Blackie in Kincorth
Hutcheon	Katherine	1710	1720	In Forrestrie (Darnaway), on Poor List
Keith	Margaret	1710		In Grangegreen, married woman aged about 40, witness against Colin Leal
Kemp	James	1710	1716	In Forrestrie, on Poor List, his funeral cost £1/10/0d in 1716
Kinnaird	Isabel	1710		In Brodie, on Poor List
Kinnaird	Isabel	1710		In Moy, on Poor List
Leal	Gilbert	1710		In Kintessack, antenuptual fornication with Isobel Rait
Leal	James	1710	1711	In Grangegreen, Servant to James Fordyce, unmarried aged about 30, witness against Colin Leal
Leal	John	1710		In Moy, aged about 60, witness against the salmon fishers
Lyon	Agnes	1710	1720	In Grangegreen, on Poor List

Malcolm	Alexander	1710		In Grangegreen, illiterate aged about 24, unmarried, witness against Colin Leal
Malcolm	Francis	1710		In Grangegreen, illiterate aged about 60, witness against Colin Leal
Man	Margaret	1710		In Dyke, on Poor List
McReadie	John	1710		In Cottartown, in antenuptial fornication with Jean Thomson
Miln	Hugh	1710		In Dyke, on Poor List
Moir	Alexander	1710	1715	In Brodie, on Poor List
Murdoch	David	1710		Servant to James Fordyce in Grangegreen, censured for scandalous carriage
Nicol	Jean	1710	1715	In Brodie, on Poor List
Ogilvie	Robert	1710		In fornication with Bessie Kerrue from Rafford
Peterkin	David	1710	1726	Salmon fisher in Lake, fished on Sabbath
Purse	Margaret	1710	1715	On Poor List, funeral cost 10/0d in 1715
Pyper	Gilbert	1710	1715	In Grangegreen, on Poor List
Pyper	Isobell	1710	1720	In Grangegreen, on Poor List
Rait	Isobel	1710		In Kintessack, in fornication with Gilbert Leal
Ross	Janet	1710	1720	In Moy, on Poor List
Ross	John	1710	1715	A lame man, on Poor List, given £4 to buy a horse in 1713
Scot	Jean	1710		On Poor List
Shearer	Wiliam	1710		On Poor List
Simpson	Elspet	1710		On Poor List
Smith	Isabel	1710		On Poor List
Souter	Alexander	1710		In Grangegreen, married man aged about 60, witness against Colin Leal, Died in the same year
Thomson	Bessie	1710	1715	In Findornhill, on Poor List
Thomson	Isabel	1710	1730	In Brodie, on poor List
Thomson	Jean	1710		In Cottartown, in antenuptial fornication with John McReadie
Tolmie	John	1710		In Grangegreen, illiterate aged about 40, witness against Colin Leal
Troup	Colin	1710		In Moy, bought trees felled in Moy Kirkyard
Troup	Jean	1710		In Grangegreen, widow aged about 40, witness against Colin Leal
Urquhart	Alexander	1710		In Grangegreen, unmarried aged about 20, witness against Colin Leal
Urquhart	Jean	1710		In Grangegreen, illiterate aged about 24, witness against Colin Leal
Urquhart	Lillias	1710	1715	In Moy, on Poor List
Urquhart	Margaret	1710	1720	In Grangegreen, on Poor List
Waxter	Elspet	1710		In Dyke, on poor List
Williamson	Alexander	1710		In Muirhall

Williamson	Margaret	1710		In Grangegreen, relict of Alexander Suter, repaid his bond th Kirk Session
Young	James	1710	1726	Salmon fisher in Moy, fished on Sabbath
Young	Margaret	1710		In Forrestrie, on Poor List
Allan	Barbara	1711		In Moy Carse, unmarried aged about 24, witness against David Peterkin
Aynwell	Christian	1711		In Moy Carse, unmarried aged about 26, witness against David Peterkin
Bluntach	John	1711	1715	In Delpottie, son to Robert Bluntach, assaulted Alexander Tolmie in 1713, in fornication with Elspet Malcolm in 1715
Bluntach	Robert	1711	1713	In Delpottie, father of John Bluntach, censured for drinking on Sabbath
Campbell	John	1711		In Moy Carse, gave in a complaint against David Peterkin
Christie	Henry	1711		In Tearie, in fornication with his servant Jean Lorrimer
Cumming	Barbara	1711		In Moy Carse, married aged about 22, witness against David Peterkin
Donaldson	Bessie	1711		In Moy Carse, married aged about 28, witness against David Peterkin
Dunbar	Anne	1711		Midwife and Ale-seller in Kintessack
Dunbar	George	1711		Alehouse owner in Kintessack
Duncan	Janet	1711	1712	Wife of David Peterkin, both were censured for slandering John Campbell
Falconer	William	1711		In Carsebanks, had his gun stolen by Alexander Taylor
Fraser	James	1711		In Cottartown, father of child by Margarett McLalland
Hay	Janet	1711	1713	Servant to James Fordyce in Grangegreen, with child by William Taylor
Hay	John	1711		Antenuptual fornication with Margaret Williamson
Lie	George	1711		In Hill of Findhorn, drinking on Sabbath
Lorrimer	Jean	1711		Servant in Tearie, in fornication with Henry Christie
McFeadle	John	1711		Witness against John Russell
McLalland	Margaret	1711		In Cottartown, with child by James Fraser
McMichael	William	1711		In fornication with Christian Smith
McQuibbans	William	1711		Witness against John Russell
Nicol	Janet	1711		In Moy Carse, widow aged about 50, witness against David Peterkin
Ogilvie	Jean	1711	1712	In Dyke, in fornication with Alexander Stuart
Ogilvy	Agnes	1711		Servant to James Fordyce in Grangegreen, censured
Peterkin	Bessie	1711		Servant to Brodie, with child by James Peterkin

Peterkin	David	1711		In Moy Carse, slandered John Campbell
Peterkin	James	1711	1716	Servant to Brodie, fathered children by Bessie Peterkin and Margaret Laing, amongst others. In 1715 described as "a contumacious adulterer", excommunicated 23rd December 1716
Russell	John	1711		In fornication with Katherine Vass
Sinclair	Alexander	1711		In Moy, drinking on Sabbath
Smith	Christian	1711		In Moy Carse, married aged about 60, witness against David Peterkin
Strachan	James	1711		In Moy Carse, unmarried aged about 18, witness against David Peterkin
Stuart	Alexander	1711		In fornication with Jean Ogilvie
Sutherland	David	1711		Servant to James Fordyce in Grangegreen, censured
Sutor	Peter	1711		In Lake, threatened with a gun by Alexander Taylor, also censured for drinking on the Sabbath
Taylor	Alexander	1711		In Hill of Findhorn, stole gun from William Falconer's house and used it to threaten Peter Sutor
Taylor	Isabel	1711		In Moy Carse, married aged about 50, witness against David Peterkin
Thomson	Peter	1711		Alehouse owner in Dyke
Vass	Katherine	1711		In fornication with John Russell
Williamson	Margaret	1711		Antenuptual fornication with John Hay
Williamson	Robert	1711		In Moy Carse, unmarried aged about 28, witness against David Peterkin
Allan	James	1712	1714	In Brodie, Kirk Elder
Black	Alexander	1712		In Wellhill, censured for scandalous behaviour, beating and scolding
Bremner	Janet	1712		In Wellhill, censured for scandalous behaviour, beating and scolding, wife of Alexander Black (above)
Callum	Isabell	1712		In Cottartown, her marriage deferred, later cancelled due to her suspected adultery with a man in Auldearn
Couper	Peter	1712	1732	In Kintessack, Kirk Elder, bought seat in north side of Wester Loft in the Kirk in 1729
Dick	James	1712	1714	In Moy, Kirk Elder
Dunbar	Elizabeth	1712		Daughter to Sir Robert Dunbar of Grangehill, her testament dated 1712
Edie	Isabel	1712		In Brodie, with child by George Findlater
Findlater	Alexander	1712		In Brodie, father to George Findlater
Findlater	Alexander	1712		In Dyke, resigned as Kirk Treasurer due to old age and infirmity
Findlater	George	1712		In Brodie, father of child by Isabel Edie
Findlater	William	1712		In fornication with Christian Waxter

Geddes	Alexander	1712		In Tearie, Kirk Elder
Gowie	Robert	1712	1714	In Easterbin, Kirk Elder
McMichael	William	1712		Antenuptual fornication with Agnes Ogilvie
Ogilvie	Agnes	1712		Antenuptual fornication with William McMichael
Paterson	William	1712		In Muirhall, drove horses on Sabbath
Smith	John	1712		In Cottartown, his marriage to Isabel Callum cancelled due to her adultery
Tolmie	William	1712	1713	"His woman" censured for Breach of Sabbath
Walker	William	1712	1714	In Earnhill, Kirk Elder, sometime Ruling Elder
Waxter	Christian	1712		In fornication with Wilima Findlater
Wilson	John	1712		In Moy, Kirk Elder
Bain	William	1713		In Carsebanks, abused William Walker
Barber	James	1713	1719	Father of Janet Barber (below)
Barber	Janet	1713	1719	Daughter to James Barber, had children by William Tolmie and John Hardie
Baxter	Peter	1713		In Moy, fished on Sabbath
Bremner	Janet	1713		Censured for cursing
Christie	Elspet	1713		Fought over a seat in the kirk
Gowdie	John	1713		In Grangegreen, given 8/0d aid by KS
Grant	Roderick	1713		His coffin cost 6/0d in 1713
Hardie	John	1713		Apprentice to John Moir in Dyke, father of child by Janet Barber
Hay	Janet	1713		In fornication with William Taylor
Henry	Magdalen	1713		Censured for cursing
Kay	Jean	1713		In fornication with George Smith
Laing	Margaret	1713	1714	In Brodie, with child by James Peterkin, stood in sackcloth each Sabbath March to July 1714
Mill	Hugh	1713		His funeral cost 8/0d in 1713
Miller	Mary	1713		Servant to Peter Thomson in Dyke, with child by Peter Sanders
Moir	John	1713		In Dyke
Peterkin	Janet	1713	1714	Fought over seat in the kirk, also censured for gathering hips and berries on the Sabbath
Sanders	Peter	1713		In fornication with Mary Miller
Smith	George	1713		In fornication with Jean Kay
Tailor	Elspet	1713		In Grangegreen, with child, censured
Taylor	Alexander	1713		In Moy, fished on Sabbath
Taylor	William	1713		In fornication with Janet Hay
Thomson	Peter	1713		In Moy, fished and also gleaned pease on Sabbath
Thomson	Robert	1713		In Moy, fished on Sabbath
Tolmie	Alexander	1713		Son to Peter Tolmie in Leyhill, assaulted by John Bluntach
Tolmie	Peter	1713		In Leyhill, father to Alexander Tolmie

Urquhart	Elspet	1713		Servant in Wester Moy, with child by Robert Young
Walker	William	1713		In Carsebanks, abused by William Bain
Young	Robert	1713		In Moy Carse, father of child by Elspet Urquhart in Wester Moy
Blackie	Isobell	1714		Fought with Bessie Urquhart
Carrack	Isobell	1714		Gathered hips and berries on Sabbath
Chalmers	James	1714		Minister of Dyke
Findlater	Alexander	1714		Kirk Elder
Findlater	William	1714		Stood in sackcloth each Sabbath March to July 1714
Gilzean	Janet	1714		Gathered hips and berries on Sabbath
Glass	Thomas	1714		In fornication with Elspet Waxter
Gowans	Christian	1714		Gathered hips and berries on Sabbath
Hay	Isobell	1714		In Wellhill, with child by Alexander Blackie for second time
Urquhart	Bessie	1714		Fought with Isobel Blackie
Waxter	Elspet	1714		In fornication with Thomas Glass, stood in sackcloth each Sabbath March to July 1714
Bluntach	Janet	1715		In Moy, on Poor List
Burry	Jean	1715		In Forrestrie, on Poor List
Carrach	John	1715		In Forrestrie, on Poor List
Christie	Christian	1715	1716	In Wellhill, on Poor List, funeral cost £1 in 1716
Clark	John	1715		In Brodie, on Poor List
Dunbar	Janet	1715	1716	In Forrestrie, on Poor List, funeral cost 12/0d in January 1716
Dunbar	Jean	1715	1716	In Dyke, in fornication with Robert Gowie
Findlay	Margaret	1715		In Brodie, on Poor List
Gowie	John	1715		In Forrestrie, on Poor List
Gowie	Robert	1715	1716	In Dyke, in fornication with Jean Dunbar
Grant	Jean	1715		In Forrestrie, on Poor List
Kinnaird	Isobell	1715		In Brodie, on Poor List
Lee	Colin	1715		In Grangegreen, on Poor List
Malcolm	Elspet	1715		In fornication with John Bluntach
Riach	Beatrice	1715		In Brodie, on Poor List
Shepherd	Helen	1715	1727	In Grangegreen, on Poor List
Simson	Elspet	1715		In Brodie, on Poor List
Smith	Christian	1715	1720	In Brodie, on Poor List
Smith	Isobell	1715		In Grangegreen, on Poor List
Smith	John	1715	1720	In Cottartown, on Poor List
Smith	Robert	1715		In Findornhill, on Poor List
Stuart	John	1715		In Brodie, on Poor List
Thomson	Janet	1715		Schoolmistress in Findornhill, salary £1 quarterly
Waxter	Christian	1715		In Forrestrie, on Poor List
Cunningham	James	1716		Witness against James Findlay, miller
Dunbar	Archibald	1716		In Grangegreen, employed James

Dunbar	Robert	1716		Findlay as miller there Witness against James Findlay, miller
Fimister	James	1716		In Wellhill, fished for salmon on Sabbath
Findlay	James	1716		Miller in Grangegreen, operated his mill on the Sabbath
Forsyth	John	1716		In Moy, fished for salmon on Sabbath
Forsyth	John	1716		In Grangegreen, husband to Jean Urquhart
Gowrie	Robert	1716		In Dyke, left 100 merks to Poor's Fund
Hay	Bessie	1716		Wife of James Findlay, miller in Grangegreen
Leal	John	1716		In Kincorth, fished for salmon on Sabbath
Murdoch	Isobell	1716		Antenuptual fornication with Alexr Roy
Peterkin	John	1716		Antenuptual fornication with Bessie Thomson
Petrie	James	1716		In Wellhill, fished for salmon on Sabbath
Robertson	Jean	1716		Servant to Chamberlain Russell in Earlsmill, accused of child murder
Ross	Isabel	1716		In Fedden, servant to, and with child by Robert Torrie
Roy	Alexander	1716		Antenuptual fornication with Isobell Murdoch
Smith	Christian	1716		Took over as teacher at Findornhill
Thomson	Bessie	1716		Antenuptual fornication with John Peterkin
Tolmie	David	1716		Witness against James Findlay, miller
Torrie	Robert	1716		In Fedden, father of child by Isabel Ross
Urquhart	Jean	1716		In Wellhill, wife of John Forsyth, censured for cursing
Bell	James	1717		In fornication with Bessie Russell
Chrystie	Margaret	1717		In Darnaway, with child by John McCarter
Clark	John	1717		In Darklass, given £4 aid to buy drugs
Dunbar	Alexander	1717	1724	Brother German to Laird of Grangehill
Dunbar	John	1717		Messenger in Dyke
Falconer	David	1717		Son to Nicol Falconer in Tearie, in scandal with Grizel Murray
Falconer	Nicol	1717		In Tearie, father of David Falconer
Fraser	Thomas	1717		Censured for bleaching on Sabbath
Hardie	John	1717		In Blackhill, antenuptual fornication with Jean Mill
Innes	Margaret	1717	1718	Servant to David Tolmie in Dyke, with child, also censured for Breach of Sabbath
Lee	Alexander	1717	1757	Kirk Elder and Kirk Treasurer in Whitemyres, his testament dated 1757
Maitland	William	1717	1720	In Dyke, admitted as Schoolmaster, Session Clerk and Precenter 17th Nov 1717, demitted office in 1720

Surname	Given	Year	Year2	Note
McCarter	John	1717		Servant to Alexander Dunbar in Grangegreen, father of child by Margaret Chrystie
Mill	Jean	1717		In Blackhill, antenuptual fornication with John Hardie
Moir	Isobell	1717		Wife to Thomas Fraser in Dyke
Murray	Grizel	1717		In Tearie, scandal with David Falconer
Nicol	Alexander	1717		Attacked by David Torrie in Whitemyres
Philp	Alexander	1717		Demitted office as Schoolmaster and Session Clerk 11 October 1717
Ross	John	1717	1720	A dumb man in Grangegreen, on Poor List, given 6/0d additional aid
Russell	Bessie	1717		In fornication with James Bell
Tolmie	David	1717		In Dyke
Torrie	David	1717		Servant to Alexander Lee in Whitemyres, struck Alexander Nicol
Alves	John	1718	1728	Teacher of the Charity School in Kintessack, on £9 a year salary, later given a pay rise
Christie	Margaret	1718		In fornication with John McArthur
Davidson	Anne	1718		Censured for Breach of Sabbath
Dunbar	William	1718		Servant to Grangehill, in fornication with Janet Scot
MacLachlan	Alexander	1718		In Darklass, in fornication with Christian Waxter
McArthur	John	1718		In fornication with Margaret Christie
McPherson	Isabel	1718		In fornication with James Peterkin, an excommunicat man
Milne	Katharine	1718		In fornication with James Reit
Reit	James	1718		In fornication with Katharine Milne
Scot	Janet	1718	1727	In Grangegreen, in fornication with William Dunbar, Mathew Baker and Hugh MackIndeen in 1727
Waxter	Christian	1718		In Darklass, in fornication with Alexander MacLachlan
Anderson	Elizabeth	1719		Antenuptual fornication with William Anderson
Anderson	William	1719		Antenuptual fornication with Elizabeth Anderson
Brodie	James	1719		In Brodie, Kirk Elder
Cameron	Grizel	1719		In fornication with William Findlater
Clark	William	1719		In Moy, Breach of Sabbath
Cumming	Alexander	1719		In Whitemyres, Kirk Elder
Demster	Henret	1719		Wife of John Leal, Breach of Sabbath
Dunbar	Ludovick	1719		In Moy, Kirk Elder
Duncan	Alexander	1719		In Moy, Breach of Sabbath
Findlater	William	1719		In fornication with Grizel Cameron
Laird	Hugh	1719		In Moy, Breach of Sabbath
Leal	John	1719		Breach of Sabbath
Lee	Alexander	1719	1732	In Moy, Kirk Elder

Maver	Alexander	1719	1752	In Earnhill, Kirk Elder
McCulloch	David	1719	1752	In Darnaway, Kirk Elder
Tolmie	William	1719		In fornication with Janet Barber
Anderson	Donald	1720		In Brodie, on Poor List
Balmano	Janet	1720		In Darklass, complained about for her unchristian expressions
Baxter	Andrew	1720		In Grangegreen, on Poor List
Bell	John	1720		In Forrestrie, on Poor List
Bremner	Bessie	1720		In Brodie, on Poor List
Brown	John	1720		Married man in scandalous conversation with Katherine Reid
Chisholme	Jean	1720		In Grangegreen, on Poor List
Cunningham	Margaret	1720		Made complaint against Janet Balmano
Dick	Alexander	1720		Admitted as Schoolmaster, Session Clerk and Precentor
Dick	Margaret	1720		In Grangegreen, on Poor List
Fraser	Kathrain	1720		In Forrestrie, on Poor List
Leal	James	1720		In Grangegreen, on Poor List
McBeth	Janet	1720		In Brodie, on Poor List
Milne	Christian	1720		In Grangegreen, on Poor List
Milne	Margaret	1720		In Grangegreen, on Poor List
Reid	Katherine	1720		In scandalous conversation with John Brown
Smith	Alexander	1720		In Brodie, on Poor List
Smith	James	1720		In Darklass, made complaint against Janet Balmano
Young	Jean	1720		In Grangegreen, on Poor List
Gordon	James	1722		From Grange in Banffshire, admitted as Schoolmaster, Session Clerk and Precentor November 1722
Turing	Alexander	1722		Demitted office as Schoolmaster, Session Clerk and Precentor November 1722
Baker	Mathew	1723	1727	In fornication with Janet Scot
Bower	William	1723		Called as witness by Kirk Session but too drunk to remember the events
Brodie	David	1723	1724	Sponsor for the baptism of John Fraser's illegitimate child. In 1724, a married man aged about 40, called as witness against the cursers
Dick	James	1723		In Moy, fished for salmon on Sabbath
Drowton	Isobell	1723		Unable to produce evidence of marriage to William McBeth
Dunbar	John	1723		In Moy, fished for salmon on Sabbath
Dunbar	William	1723		In Kincorth, in uncleanness with Sarah Stewart
Findlater	William	1723		In Dyke, excommunicated for his repeated fornications with Isobel Hay
Fraser	John	1723		Allowed to have illegitimate child baptised

McBeth	William	1723		Unable to produce evidence of marriage to Isobell Drowton
McKay	George	1723		In Moy, fished for salmon on Sabbath
Nicolson	Alexander	1723		In Moy, fished for salmon on Sabbath
Stewart	Sarah	1723		In Kincorth, in uncleanness with William Dunbar
Young	John	1723	1726	In Moy, fished for salmon on Sabbath
Austie	Alexander	1724		In Moy, granted a testimonial
Cunningham	Margaret	1724		Unmarried, aged about 18, witness against the cursers
Duncan	Elizabeth	1724		Unmarried, aged about 40, witness against the cursers
Edie	Kathrin	1724		Censured for cursing
Forsyth	John	1724		In Grangegreen, censured for employing William Findlater an excommunicat man
Gairn	William	1724		Tenant at the Miln of Moy
Gowie	James	1724		Granted a testimonial
Henderson	John	1724		In Kintessack, cohabited with Grizel Smith, she now with child
Kemp	Kathryn	1724		In Tearie, censured for employing William Findlater an excommunicat man
McKenzie	Ann	1724		Granted a testimonial
Milne	John	1724		In Blackhill, censured for employing William Findlater an excommunicat man
Smith	Grizel	1724		In Kintessack, cohabited with John Henderson, now with child
Stewart	Margaret	1724	1726	Widow in Moy, aged about 60, witness against the cursers
Storm	John	1724	1726	In Moy, witness against the fishers
Tolmie	Christian	1724		In Longhill, daughter to Peter Tolmie and Isobel Williamson, troubled by William Findlater, an excommunicat man
Tolmie	Peter	1724		In Longhill, father of Christian Tolmie
Torrie	Girsel	1724		Censured for cursing
Williamson	Isobel	1724		Wife to Peter Tolmie

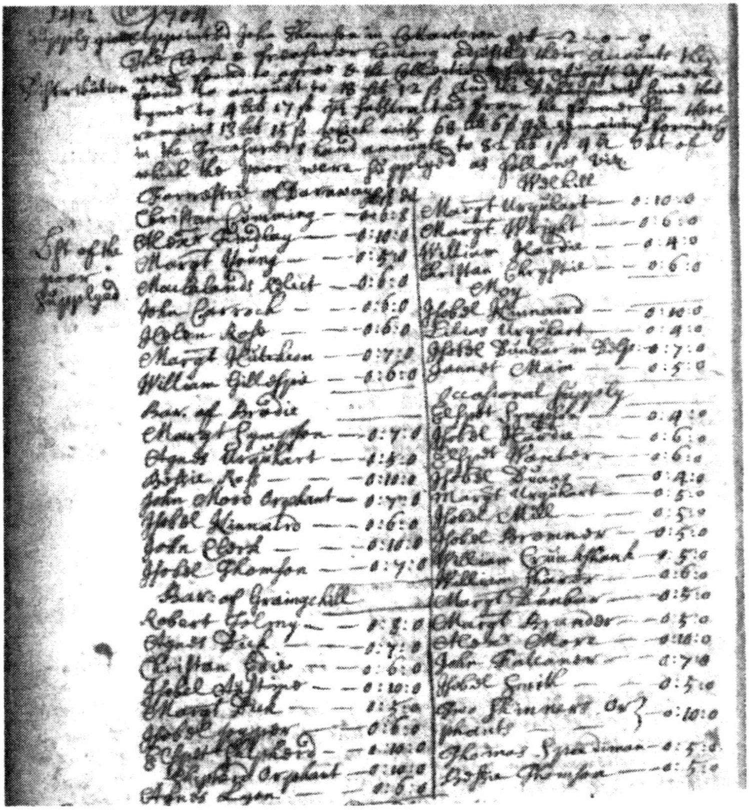

1709

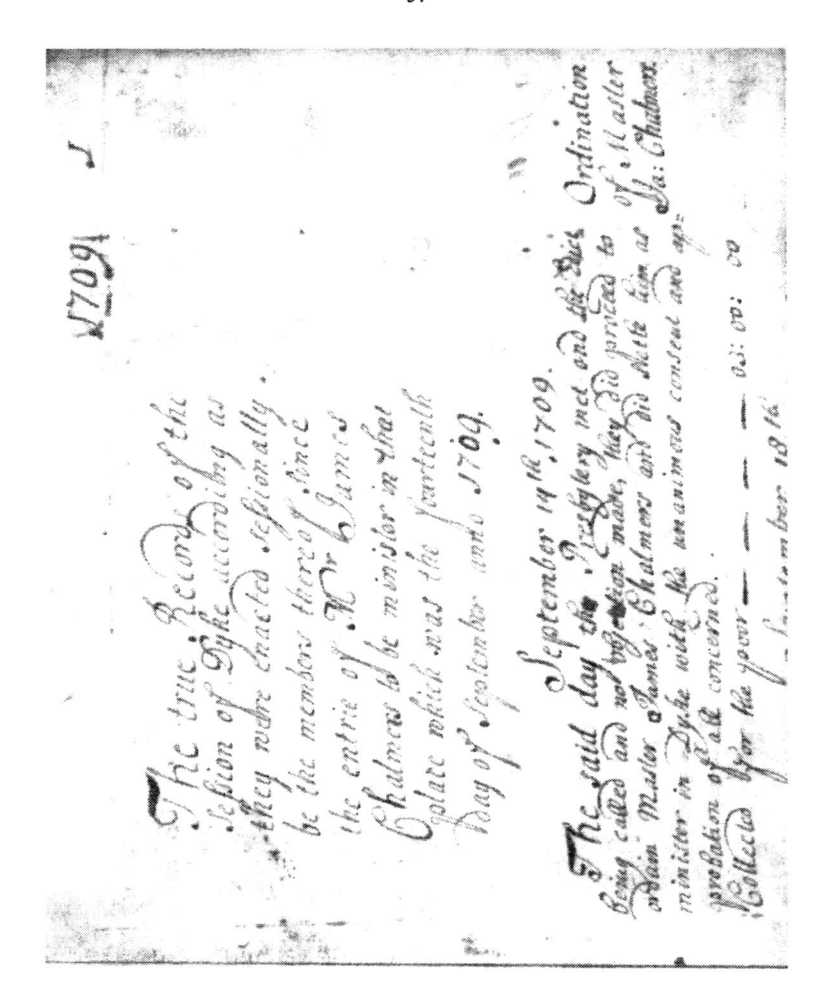

The true Record of the Session of Dyke according as they were enacted sessionally, be the members thereof since the entrie of Mr James Chalmers to be minister in that place which was the fourteenth day of September 1709.

September 14th, 1709. The said day the Presbytery met and did this Ordination being called and no Infor=mation made, they Proceided to Of Master Adam Master James Chalmers and did state him as Ja: Chalmers minister in Dyke with the unanimous consent and ap= probation of all concerned.

Collected for the poor — — — [illegible] 00: 00

September 18th

Chapter 5

The Parish of Dyke and Moy from 1725 to 1749

William Falconer applied to be released from his excommunication early in 1725, so that he could have his child baptized. This seems to have eventually been agreed. John Grant and Ann Davidson, now in Edinkillie, were excommunicated for their incest, *"and this congregation was inhibit any unnecessary converse with them"*. John Martin in Bogs represented to the Session that Kathrin Hardie, lately buried, had nothing to defray the funeral charges, and as she was owed money by John Dunbar in Netherwaterside and by Isobel Hasbin in Dyke these debts could be collected to pay for the funeral expenses.

In 1726 many of the events of the parish were overshadowed in the Session Minutes by the Minister's removal to Aberdeen. Alexander Nicolson was the Ruling Elder, and Alexander Lee was continued as an Elder. The new minister, Robert Dunbar of Ballinspink, was installed during the year. He was married to Jean Miller from Edinburgh, and he served the parish until his death on 23rd April 1782. The fishers were, as usual, in trouble, and David Peterkin and James Peterkin in Lake, John and James Young [again], Alexander Hays elder and younger in Grangegreen, Robert Speediman and John Scott all received censure for breach of Sabbath. They finally confessed their sins the following year. John Dunbar was chosen as Ruling Elder in 1727.

John Alves, the Charity Schoolmaster in Kintessack, represented in 1728 that his salary was so small that *"he can scarce support his family and attend the business of the school"*. He was given £3 pending a decision by the Session about his salary. Alexander Gowie, the Kirk Officer, also asked for an increase in his salary at this time. Robert McMichel and Cathrin Williamson, having not appeared before the Session, were declared to be fugitives from Kirk discipline.

1729 saw the allocation of the seats in the new Wester Loft of the kirk, the south side seats going to Alexander Fraser in Berryley, Robert Balmanno in Boggs, James Jack in Moy, William Bremner in Tearie, John Young in Muirhall and William Bower in Cottertown. The north side seats went to Hary Christie in Tarie, Collin Hardie in Dyke, Peter Couper in Kintessack, John Bluntach in Delpottie, David Tulloch in Binsness and Peter Hardie in Wellhill. The groups of seats allocated would depend on the size of each of the families.

James Garden and Isobel Fordice were rebuked for their irregular marriage in 1730, but were then declared married by the minister. Alexander Nicolson was continued as Ruling Elder for the next two years, and testificats were granted to John Black, George Lee and James Davidson.

In 1731 David Short, Collin Hardie, John Cruickshank, James Malcom, William Scot, Jean Scot, Elspet Malcom in Blackhill, Agnes Lyon in Muirtown and Isobel Paterson, a servant to Collin Hardie were all censured for breach of Sabbath as they had all been caught drinking during the time of the afternoon sermon. Henrietta Tulloch had a child in David Gowie's house, the father was Robert Fraser who was now a gardener at Novar. Kathrin Ogilvie, daughter to Robert Ogilvie in Newlands of Brodie, was with child by James Ross from the parish of Fern [probably Fearn in Ross-shire rather than Fern in Angus], the child being begotten in the garden of the mansion house of Fern. John McBeth in Earlsmill craved aid from the Kirk Session in his hardship, and a collection was taken towards creating a hospital for beggars either in the parish or elsewhere in the county.

In 1732 the Kirk Session are identified as Mr Robert Dunbar, Minister, Alexander Nicolson, John Dunbar, Peter Couper, Alexander Maver, James Dick, Donald McCulloch, Alexander Lie in Moy and Alexander Lie in Whitemyre, the latter also being Treasurer. James Dick was Ruling Elder.

Also in 1732 William Ross in Kintessack was reduced to great poverty and straits, lately sustaining such losses by the death of his horses that he was scarce able to continue in his labouring – he was given £6 in aid by the Session to buy new horses. Alexander Gowrie was given £1/4/0d to buy shoes, and the Session also paid for the funeral and coffin of Jean Birnie, one of the poor, which cost £1/15/4d.

The following year Janet Hutcheon arrived in the parish, with child by Mr Brodie, younger of Lethen, and she stayed at Tearie. George Lee in the Hill of Findhorn was given £3, being "*in poverty and straits*". A coffin and funeral was provided for Katherin Hutcheon at a cost of £1/16/0d, and Isobel Falconer was with child by James Duff, a soldier formerly based in the parish. William Gowie, the Kirk Officer, possibly the son of the former Kirk Officer Alexander Gowie, was given a salary of £11/13/4d for 18 months, together with £1/16/0d to buy shoes.

The Kirk Session Minutes for 1734 to 1737 are virtually illegible, but in 1734 there is documentary evidence of the Duff family owning much of the land of Culbin.[42] In 1738 the Session paid 3 shillings for a coffin for Bessie Lawson, and paid Anne Latto 5 shillings for keeping a school in the parish. Testificats were granted to Katherin McKay, William Ross, James Lawson and Margaret Moir.

1739 saw the appointment of John Russell as Session Clerk, and William Allan in Langley and Isobel Dunbar were cited for presumption of scandal. Robert Dunbar in Grangegreen applied to be released from his excommunication and was absolved, and testificats were granted to Alexander Smith and Isobel McMichal.

There were few events recorded in the Session minutes over the next few years, but these included James Bell younger at the Boat of Findhorn, who was censured for fishing on the Sabbath in 1740, an event witnessed by James Hoyes, Ludovick Ross and John Sutor. The following year testificats or testimonials were granted to Robert Petrie and David Murray. In 1742 David and James Peterkin in Moy Carse beat each other and were censured for breach of Sabbath.

In 1743 the wages for a male servant were generally 16/8d per half year, and for a similar period a female servant would be paid 7/8d.[43] A rape committed by a soldier at about this time was reputed to have been punished by his public execution.[44] John Forsyth was appointed a Kirk Elder, Peter Thomson was the church treasurer and

---

[42] National Archives of Scotland GD44/38/67/1 et seq
[43] Old Statistical Account for the Parish of Dyke and Moy
[44] ibid

William Gowie was the Kirk Officer. Repairs were made to the church, a new door was put into the East Gable, and glass was replaced in several of the windows, and the following year some new windows were fitted at a cost of £40/19/6d Scots.

In amongst the cases of fornication and breach of Sabbath during 1744 a case of suspected murder appears. *"Lillias Tolmie in Leyhill, a married woman whose husband has been out of this country for several years, was with child by Alexander Tolmie in Leyhill, a married man, and she had an abortion on Thursday last"*. On investigation it appeared that the child had reached full term and the case was so strong that the Kirk Session asked the Magistrate to raise a warrant for murder. The warrant for her incarceration was raised, and Janet Chalmers and Margaret Russell were called as witnesses. The record of the final outcome of the trial does not appear to have survived.

The records during 1745 and 1746 are very patchy, the Session not being able to meet regularly due to the disruption caused by the Jacobite Rebellion, and apart from a few fornications and payments for coffins there is little documentation of life in the parish during these disturbed times. It would be obvious, however, that both the Rebel Troops and Cumberland's army would have passed through the parish, and this would almost certainly have been a massive drain on the resources of the inhabitants, as happened almost everywhere along their marches.

In 1747 there was a paucity of Kirk Elders, and the new Elders were James Williamson in Fedden, William Lie in Layhill, Robert Bluntach in Wellhill, James Bluntach in Kintessack, James Wright in Hill of Findhorn and John McKay in Moy. Mrs McKay was paid £4/4/0d for teaching the young children in Blackhill and Christian Thomason was paid £22/13/4d for looking after the child of William Nicol. John Sutor, the Kirk Treasurer, recommended to the Minister that they buy 2 dozen Bibles and as many New Testaments to give to the poor children of the parish.

By 1748 the Session minutes become more complete, with numerous cases of fornication, scolding and all the usual misdemeanours of a rural Scottish parish. Robert Bluntach was now the Ruling Elder. Agnes Miller in Darklass was with child by Ralph Wilson, the smith in Dyke, and a married man, so she was immediately branded an adultress. The witnesses to this case were numerous and quite enthusiastic in their testimony. Among them were Janet Millar aged about 60, Elizabeth Bain aged 35, John McWatt aged 18, Margaret McWatt aged 19, Anne Clark aged 40, John Bower aged 'something over 30', Andrew Munro in Darklass aged over 30, Margaret Davidson, an 18-year old and Janet Munro aged 25. Polson Dawson, a married man in Moy, was censured for his scandalous behaviour with Marjory Sinclair in Moy on the banks of the Water of Findhorn, after they had each drunk several chopins of ale together in James Forsyth's house in Forres.

Jean McKay in Blackhill was with child by Walter Ross in Cannisby in Caithness. She was considered by the Session *"to be only a vagrant, and that she had brought several children into the county and never gave any evidence of her being married"*. She was made to stand in sackcloth and then she and presumably also the children were banished from the parish.

Through 1749 and 1750 very little is recorded, Robert Bluntach was still the Ruling Elder and there were a few cases of fornication, but all told it was a quiet time. In 1749 the lands of Grangehill, including the Miln of Moy, were sold in favour of Alexander Grant of Dalvey.[45] In the same year there was a payment by Alexander Brodie of Brodie to the Duke of Gordon (in right of the late Earl of Dunfermling) of the yearly feu duties of Penick and the Mill of Moynes, which amounted to 4 bolls bear, 12 capons, 12 hens and £32/15/4d, backdated to 1733. These documents[46] show that although the lands of Penick and Meikle Penick were considered to be in the parish of Dyke and Moy, they actually fell under the jurisdiction of the Lordship and Regality of Urquhart, the former lands of the Earl of Dunfermline to the east of Elgin, and were actually in the Country of Nairn. The disputes over this land continued until at least 1774.

Some of the inhabitants of Dyke and Moy from 1725 to 1749

Surname	Forename	Year	Year2	Notes
Allan	Robert	1725	1727	In Lake, in fornication with Christian Lawson
Barber	Christian	1725		In fornication with Robert Michal
Davidson	Ann	1725		Excommunicated for incest with John Grant
Dunbar	John	1725		In Netherwaterside, his debt used to pay the costs of Kathrin Hardie's funeral
Grant	John	1725		Excommunicated for his incest with Ann Davidson
Hardie	Kathrin	1725		In Boggs, 'lately buried' the money owed to her by John Dunbar and Isobell Hasbin, used to pay for her funeral
Hasbin	Isobell	1725		Her debt used to pay the costs of Kathrin Hardie's funeral
Lawson	Christian	1725	1728	In Lake, in fornication with Robert Allan in 1725 and in adultery with John Allan in 1728
Martin	John	1725		In Boggs, queried the costs of Kathrin Hardies funeral
McKater	Mary	1725		Granted a testimonial
Michal	Robert	1725		In fornication with Christian Barber
Petrie	Alexander	1725		Granted a testimonial
Waxter	Joan	1725		In fornication with Sir Harry Innes of Innes
Clerk	William	1726		In Moy, fished for salmon on Sabbath
Dunbar	Robert	1726	1782	Of Ballinspink, lived in Dyke, Minister and later Trustee of the Women's School of Dyke
Hardie	John	1726		In Moy, fished for salmon on Sabbath
Hay	Alexander	1726		In Grangegreen, fished for salmon on Sabbath

---

[45] National Archives of Scotland GD44/24/21
[46] National Archives of Scotland GD44/24/37

Kemp	John	1726		In Kintessack, his daughter with child by an unknown man
Peterkin	James	1726		In Moy, fished for salmon on Sabbath
Scot	John	1726		In Moy, fished for salmon on Sabbath
Speediman	Robert	1726		In Moy, fished for salmon on Sabbath
Tulloch	Jean	1726		Granted a testimonial
Austie	Thomas	1727		In Wellhill, given aid by Kirk Session
Brodie	William	1727		In Cormackshill, given aid by Kirk Session
Findlay	James	1727		In Moy Carse, given aid by Kirk Session
Hutcheon	James	1727		In Whitemyres, given aid by Kirk Session
Innes	Margaret	1727		In Delpottie, given aid by Kirk Session
MackIndeen	Hugh	1727		In fornication with Janet Scot
Ogilvie	Hugh	1727		Antenuptual fornication with Kathrin Urquhart
Urquhart	Kathrin	1727		Antenuptual fornication with Hugh Ogilvie
Allan	John	1728		In adultery with Christian Lawson
Falconer	Isobell	1728		In fornication with James Harper
Gowie	Alexander	1728		Kirk Officer, asked for pay rise in 1728
Harper	James	1728		In fornication with Isobell Falconer
McMichal	Robert	1728		Fugitive from Kirk Discipline
Williamson	Cathrin	1728		Fugitive from Kirk Discipline
Balmanno	Robert	1729		In Boggs, had seat in Wester Loft of Kirk, south side
Bluntach	John	1729		In Delpottie, had seat in Wester Loft of Kirk, north side
Bower	William	1729		In Cottartown of Brodie, had seat in Wester Loft of Kirk, south side
Christie	Hary	1729		In Tearie, had seat in Wester Loft of Kirk, north side
Forsyth	Isobell	1729		In Grangegreen, antenuptual fornication with Alexander Hay
Fraser	Alexander	1729		In Berryley, had seat in Wester Loft of Kirk, south side
Fraser	Margaret	1729		In Earnhill, now gone to Rafford, in fornication with John Ross
Hardie	Colin	1729	1731	In Dyke, had seat in Wester Loft of Kirk, north side. Also censured for drinking on the Sabbath
Hardie	Robert	1729		In Wellhill, had seat in Wester Loft of Kirk, north side
Hay	Alexander	1729		In Grangegreen, antenuptual fornication with Isobel Forsyth
Jack	James	1729		In Moy, had seat in Wester Loft of Kirk, south side
Milne	John	1729		In Blackhill, paid off his £1 bill (debt) to the Kirk Session
Ogilvie	George	1729		In Tearie, given £1/4/0d aid by Kirk

Ross	John	1729		Session In Earnhill, in fornication with Margaret Fraser
Tulloch	David	1729		In Binsness, had seat in Wester Loft of Kirk, north side
Young	John	1729		In Muirhall, had seat in Wester Loft of Kirk, south side
Black	John	1730		Granted a testimonial
Davidson	James	1730		Granted a testimonial
Fordyce	Isobell	1730		Irregular marriage to James Garden solemnised by the minister
Garden	James	1730		Irregular marriage to Isobell Fordyce solemnised by the minister
Lee	George	1730		Granted a testimonial
Lyon	Agnes	1730	1731	In Muirtown, given aid by Kirk Session despite being censured for drinking on the Sabbath
Pyper	Isobell	1730		In Muirtown, given aid by Kirk Session
Young	John	1730		In Findhornhill, given aid by Kirk Session
Cruickshank	John	1731	1733	Servant in Grangegreen, censured for drinking on Sabbath, also in fornication with Jean Scot. Granted a testimonial in 1733
Malcolm	Elspet	1731		In Blackhill, drinking on Sabbath
Malcolm	James	1731		In Dyke, drinking on Sabbath
McBeth	John	1731		In Earlsmill, given aid by Krik Session
Ogilvie	Kathrin	1731		Daughter to Robert Ogilvie in Newlands of Brodie, with child by James Ross from Fern
Pantoun	Isobell	1731		Censured for drinking on Sabbath
Scot	Jean	1731		In Dyke, censured for drinking on Sabbath
Scot	William	1731		Censured for drinking on Sabbath
Short	David	1731		Censured for drinking on Sabbath
Tulloch	Henrietta	1731		Had child by Robert Fraser now in Novar
Bremner	Kathrin	1732		With child by John Lamb
Campbell	James	1732	1733	Given aid by Kirk Session, testimonial in 1733
Dick	James	1732		Kirk Elder
Laird	John	1732	1758	Kirk Elder
Lamb	John	1732	1748	Father of child by Kathrin Bremner, later granted a testimonial
Muirson	Thomas	1732	1758	In Tearie, Kirk Elder
Ross	William	1732		In Kintessack, reduced to poverty by the death of his horses, given £6 by Kirk Session to buy new horse
Scot	Jean	1732		In Grangegreen, in fornication with John Cruickshank

Spence	Anna	1732		In Grangegreen, with child by John Baillie in Inverness
Bluntach	John	1733		In Moy, father of child by Bessie Nicol
Clerk	Margaret	1733		Antenuptual fornication with Alexander Suter
Clerk	Thomas	1733		In Brodie, father of child by Janet Dunbar
Duff	John	1733	1741	of Culbin
Dunbar	Janet	1733		In Brodie, with child by Thomas Clerk
Falconer	Isabel	1733		With child by James Duff, a soldier
Gowie	William	1733	1743	Kirk Officer, salary £11/13/4d for 18 months, also given £1/16/0d for shoes
Hutcheon	Janet	1733		In Tearie, with child by Mr Brodie younger of Lethen
Nicol	Bessie	1733		In Moy, with child by John Bluntach
Nicolson	Isobell	1733		Antenuptual fornication with James Speediman
Russell	James	1733		Antenuptual fornication with Elspet Simson
Simson	Elspet	1733		Antenuptual fornication with James Russell
Speediman	James	1733		Antenuptual fornication with Isobell Nicolson
Suter	Alexander	1733		Antenuptual fornication with Margaret Clerk
Burry	John	1737		In Whitemyres, on Poor List
Hendry	Alexander	1737		In Whitemyres, on Poor List
Leal	Margaret	1737		In Blackhill, on Poor List
Piper	William	1737		In Kintessack, on Poor List
Pledger	John	1737		On Poor List
Hosack	Helen	1738		Servant to Bailie Hosack, with child by Ludovick Kay
Kay	Ludovick	1738		Father of child by Helen Hosack
Latto	Anna	1738		Paid salary of 5/0d by Kirk Session for keeping a school at Dyke
Lawson	Bessie	1738		Her coffin cost 3/0d
Lawson	James	1738		Granted a testimonial
McKay	Katherine	1738		Granted a testimonial
McPherson	Elizabeth	1738	1745	In Whitemyres, had children by Alexander Robertson
Moir	Margaret	1738		Granted a testimonial
Robertson	Alexander	1738	1745	Father of children by Elizabeth McPherson
Ross	William	1738		Granted a testimonial
Allan	Anna	1739		In Longley, aged about 18, witness against William Allan
Allan	Janet	1739		In Longley, aged about 20, witness against William Allan
Allan	William	1739	1742	In Longley, censured for scandal with Isobel Dunbar in 1739

Cattanach	Elspet	1739		In Darnaway, alias McIntosh, servant to John Davidson, with child by Alexander Davidson
Clunas	David	1739	1740	In Blackhill, father of a child by Margaret Peterkin, complained against her for false accusations
Davidson	Alexander	1739		In Darnaway, father of child by Elspet Cattanach
Davidson	John	1739		In Darnaway
Dunbar	Isobel	1739		In Longley, in scandal with William Allan
Dunbar	Robert	1739		In Grangegreen, absolved from his excommunication
Frize	Mary	1739		In Longley, aged under 16, witness against William Allan
McMichal	Isobel	1739		Granted a testimonial
Peterkin	Margaret	1739	1740	In Fedden, with child by David Clunas in Blackhills
Russell	John	1739		Session Clerk
Smith	Alexander	1739		Granted a testimonial
Bell	James	1740		In Boat of Findhorn, fished on Sabbath
Brebner	Alexander	1740		In Newtown of Brodie, married man aged about 58, witness for David Clunas
Hay	John	1740		In Earnhill, his testament dated 1740
Hoyes	James	1740		In Boat of Findhorn, married man aged about 34, witness against James Bell
Lauder	Margaret	1740		In Newtown of Brodie, married woman aged about 40, witness for David Clunas
Lauder	Margaret	1740		In Fedden, married woman aged about 62, witness for David Clunas
Ross	Ludovick	1740		In Boat of Findhorn, married man aged about 35, witness against James Bell
Simson	Robert	1740		In Fedden, aged about 64, witness for David Clunas
Suter	John	1740		In Boat of Findhorn, unmarried man aged about 18, witness against James Bell
Fraser	Mary	1741		With child by Alexander McLalan
McLalan	Alexander	1741		Father of child by Mary Fraser
Murray	David	1741		Granted a testimonial
Nicol	William	1741		Antenuptual fornication with Jean Ross
Petrie	Robert	1741		Granted a testimonial
Ross	Jean	1741		Antenuptual fornication with William Nicol
Anderson	Marjory	1742		In Moy Carse, married woman aged about 30, witness against David and James Peterkin
Anderson	Robert	1742		In Moy Carse, married man aged about 60, witness against David and James Peterkin

Blackie	James	1742		In Longley
Grant	Ann	1742		Servant to James Blackie in Longley, with child by John Johnston
Johnston	John	1742		Servant to William Allan in Longley, father of child by Ann Grant
Leal	George	1742		In Moy Carse, unmarried man aged about 20, witness against David and James Peterkin
Muirson	Margaret	1742		In Moy Carse, unmarried woman aged about 16, witness against David and James Peterkin
Munro	Janet	1742		In Moy Carse, married woman aged 47, witness against David and James Peterkin
Peterkin	David	1742		Beat James Peterkin on Sabbath
Peterkin	James	1742		Beat David Peterkin on Sabbath
Tulloch	Katherine	1742		In Moy Carse, unmarried woman aged over 50, witness against David and James Peterkin
Young	Jean	1742		In Moy Carse, unmarried woman aged about 20, witness against David and James Peterkin
Davidson	James	1743		Merchant in Darnaway, his testament dated 1743
Edie	James	1743		In Grangegreen, father of child by Jean Falconer
Falconer	Jean	1743		In Grangegreen, with child by James Edie
Forsyth	John	1743	1758	In Grangegreen, Kirk Elder
Leal	Jean	1743		In Kintessack, with child by James Shearer
Mason	Alexander	1743		In Moy Carse, father of child by Isobel Nicol
Nicol	Isobel	1743		In Moy Carse, with child by Alexander Mason
Petrie	William	1743		Granted a testimonial
Ross	Ludovick	1743	1762	Farmer in Broom of Moy, mentioned in Rentals of 1762
Shearer	James	1743		In Kintessack, father of child by Jean Leal
Sinclair	Marjory	1743		In Broom of Moy, with child by Donald Reid in Ardclach
Spence	Jean	1743		Censured for adultery
Thomson	Peter	1743	1744	Kirk Elder, Treasurer and interim Session Clerk
Callum	Jean	1744		With child by David Cumming, Rafford
Chalmers	Janet	1744		In Leyhill, married woman aged about 60, witness against Lillias Tolmie
Cumming	Margaret	1744		In Wellhill, with child by John Sanders

Forsyth	Isobel	1744		In Lake, antenuptual fornication with John Frize
Fraser	John	1744		In Earlsmill, father of child by Christian McIntosh in Croy
Fraser	William	1744		In Brodie, father of child by Katherine Grant
Frize	John	1744		In Lake, antenuptual fornication with Isobel Forsyth
Grant	Katherine	1744		Servant in Brodie, with child by William Fraser
Ker	James	1744		In Newlands of Brodie
Miln	Mary	1744		Servant to Robert Watson, with child by James Murdoch
Munro	Hugh	1744		Granted a testimonial
Murdoch	David	1744	1745	In Blackhill, censured for threshing corn on Sabbath. Coffin for his wife cost £1/16/0d in 1745
Murdoch	James	1744		In Brodie, father of child by Mary Miln
Pyper	James	1744		Granted a testimonial
Russell	Margaret	1744		In Leyhill, widow aged over 40, witness against Lillias Tolmie
Sanders	John	1744		In Wellhill, father of child by Margaret Cumming
Tolmie	Alexander	1744		In Leyhill, married man, fathered child in adultery with Lillias Tolmie
Tolmie	Lillias	1744		In Leyhill, had child in adultery with Alexander Tolmie, disposed of child, accused of child murder
Barber	Katherine	1745		With child by Donald McKenzie
Leal	William	1745		Coffin for his son cost £1/16/0d
McKenzie	Donald	1745		Father of child by Katherine Barber
Campbell	Margaret	1746	1752	Servant to William Fraser in Darklass, with child by William McBeth. Granted testimonial in 1752
Fraser	William	1746	1748	In Darklass, antenuptual fornication
McBeth	William	1746		In Darklass, father of child by Margaret Campbel
Nicol	James	1746	1753	In Moy, fathered children by Margaret Peterkin and by Jean Lamb, also censured for scandalous behaviour with Margaret Hardie
Peterkin	Margaret	1746		In Moy, unmarried, with child by James Nicol
Reid	Isobel	1746		In Lake, with child by Peter Suter in Kinloss
Bluntach	James	1747	1768	Farmer in Kintessack, Kirk Elder, mentioned in rentals 1768
Bluntach	Robert	1747	1788	In Wellhill, Kirk Elder
Dollas	William	1747		In Moy, father of child by Isobell Lee
Dunbar	John	1747		In Darnaway, father of Margaret Dunbar

Dunbar	Margaret	1747		Daughter to John Dunbar (above), with child by William Gold, a Dragoon based in Darnaway
Lee	Isobell	1747		Servant to Jean Leal in Moy, with child by William Dollas, fellow servant
Lie	William	1747	1752	In Leyhill, Kirk Elder
McGregor	William	1747		In Lake, father of child by Janet Roy in Blackhill
McKay	John	1747	1752	In Moy, Kirk Elder
Roy	Janet	1747		In Blackhill, with child by William McGregor in Lake
Suter	John	1747		In Dyke, Kirk Treasurer
Sutherland	Barbara	1747		Granted a testimonial
Thomson	Christian	1747		Cared for William Nicol's child, paid £22/13/4d Scots by Kirk Session
Williamson	James	1747	1752	In Fedden, Kirk Elder
Wright	James	1747	1752	In Hill of Findhorn, Kirk Elder
Anderson	Elizabeth	1748		Antenuptual fornication with Robert Petrie
Bain	Elizabeth	1748		In Darklass, aged about 35, witness against Ralph Wilson
Bower	John	1748		In Darklass, married man aged just over 30, witness against Ralph Wilson
Buie	Elizabeth	1748		Censured for scolding
Clark	Anne	1748		In Darklass, aged about 40, witness against Ralph Wilson
Clunas	David	1748		In Tearie, married widow Jean Smith who had earlier had a child by James Clunas
Clunas	James	1748		In Tearie, father of child by widow Jean Smith
Davidson	Margaret	1748		In Darklass, aged over 18, witness against Ralph Wilson
Dawson	Polson	1748		In Moy, a married man in drunken scandal with Marjory Sinclair
Dean	Margaret	1748		Censured for scolding
Gowdie	David	1748		In Cottartown of Brodie, testimonial
McKay	Jean	1748		In Blackhill, with child by Walter Ross in Canisbay, considered by Kirk Session to be 'a vagrant with several children' and banished from the parish
McWatt	John	1748		In Darklass, unmarried aged over 18, witness against Ralph Wilson
McWatt	Margaret	1748		In Darklass, unmarried aged about 19, witness against Ralph Wilson
Millan	Janet	1748		In Darklass, aged about 60, witness against Ralph Wilson
Miller	Agnes	1748		In Darklass, with child in adultery with Ralph Wilson, a married man
Muirson	Jean	1748		In Moy Carse, with child by John Nicol

Munro	Andrew	1748		In Darklass, a married man aged over 30, witness against Ralph Wilson
Munro	Janet	1748		In Darklass, aged about 25, witness against Ralph Wilson
Nicol	John	1748		In Moy Carse, father of a child by Jean Muirson
Petrie	Robert	1748		Antenuptual fornication with Elizabeth Anderson
Shearer	Elizabeth	1748		Granted a testimonial
Sinclair	Marjory	1748		In Moy, censured for scandal with Polson Dawson when they both were drunk
Smith	David	1748		Granted a testimonial
Smith	Jean	1748		Widow in Tearie, had child by James Clunas, later that year married David Clunas
Stewart	John	1748		In Darnaway, antenuptual fornication
Stuart	Alexander	1748		Granted a testimonial
Wilson	Ralph	1748		Smith in Dyke, a married man, in adultery with Agnes Miller
Black	Ludovick	1749		Denied fathering a child by Isobell Kilgour
Brodie	Alexander	1749	1752	Of Brodie, Lord Lyon, Trustee of the Women's School at Dyke, paid feu duty on the lands of Meikle Pennick
Kay	James	1749		In Grangegreen, father of child by Jean Tolmie
Kilgour	Isobell	1749		With child by Ludovick Black
Moir	James	1749		His coffin cost 3/0d
Roy	Jean	1749		With child supposedly by Claud Thomson
Sutherland	William	1749		Servant in Dyke, fathered child by Mary Watson, fellow servant
Thomson	Claud	1749		Denied fathering child by Jean Roy
Tolmie	Jean	1749		In Grangegreen, with child by James Kay
Watson	Mary	1749		Servant in Dyke, with child by Willliam Sutherland, fellow servant

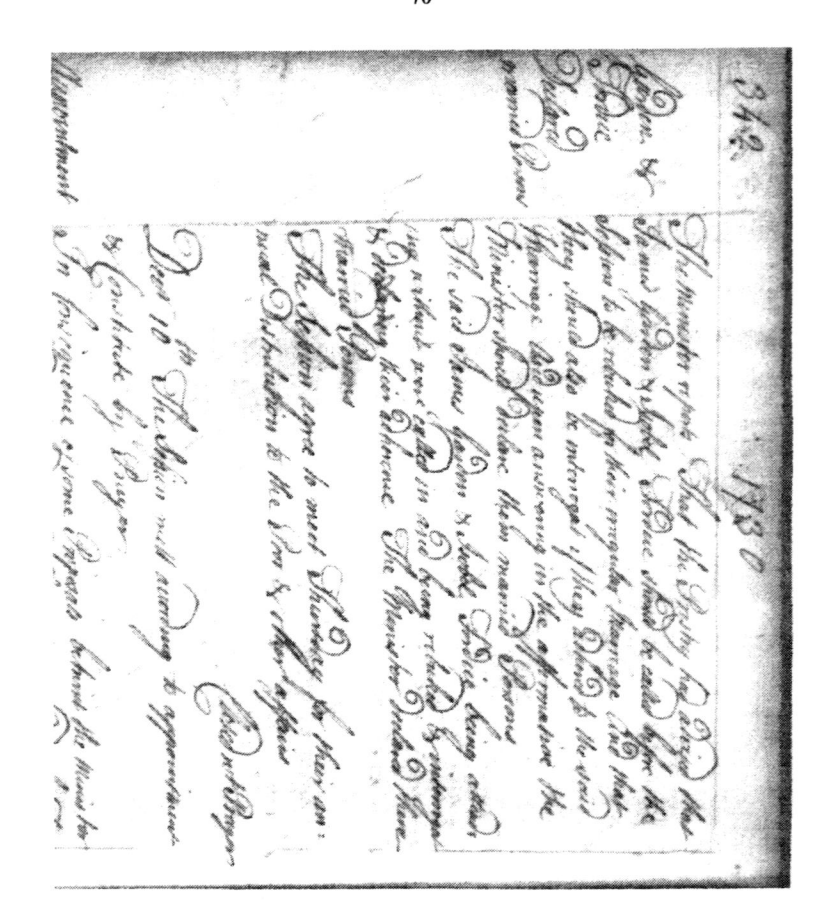

Legalisation of Irregular Marriage between James Garden and Isobel Fordice
December 1730
National Archives of Scotland CH2/779/3/343

1730

The Examination of the Treasurer Accounts being
at this time delayed The Session proceeded to distribute
Supply to the Enrolled Poor as follows

To	£ s d	To	£ s d	
James Hay	1–10–0	Janet Urquhart	0–18–0	Distribution
David Davidsons Relict	1–10–0	Helen Shepherd	1–4–0	of money
Alex Allan	0–18–0	Christian Miles	0–18–0	
David Milne	1–16–0	Jean Stendry	0–18–0	
Janet Taylor	0–18–0	Isobel Reid	0–18–0	
Katharin Hutchon	1–4–0	Jean Godsman	1–16–0	
Alex Smith of Shield	2–0–0	Wm Hardie	0–18–0	
Margaret Thomas	0–12–0	Thomas Rustic	1–10–0	
Janet Glass	0–12–0	Margaret Dunbar	1–4–0	
Christian Gerrans	1–4–0	Isobel Hendrie	1–0–0	
Janet Walker	0–12–0	Alex Lawson	1–16–0	
John Wat	1–16–0	Margaret Innes	4–4–0	
Isobel Thomson	0–0–0	John Rose	1–4–0	
James Petrikin	1–4–0	Margery Dick	1–4–0	
Helen Mikiddie	0–12–0	Jn Lake	3–0–0	
Isobel Piper	1–0–0	John Hutchan	0–18–0	
Agnes Lyon	0–18–0	Margaret Blenshu	1–4–0	
Christian Falconer	1–10–0	Isobel Duncan	1–4–0	
Janet Shepherd	0–12–0	Elspet Hutchson	1–4–0	
Janet Thomson	0–18–0	George Ogilvie	3–0–0	
	£22–2–0		£30–2–0	

Sum of both Columns is Fifty two pound 4 shilling
The Session having caused summons to this Dyet such Intimation
of the above Poor as were able to attend And Some to the Poor anent
of them concerning the Sessions late Act anent the Sessions late
leaving their effects to the Poor of the Parish in case Act
of their after Applications for Supply was intimate to
them. And the same Intimation was appointed to be
made at Delivering the Proportions to Such as are now
absent

Will Grant Clk

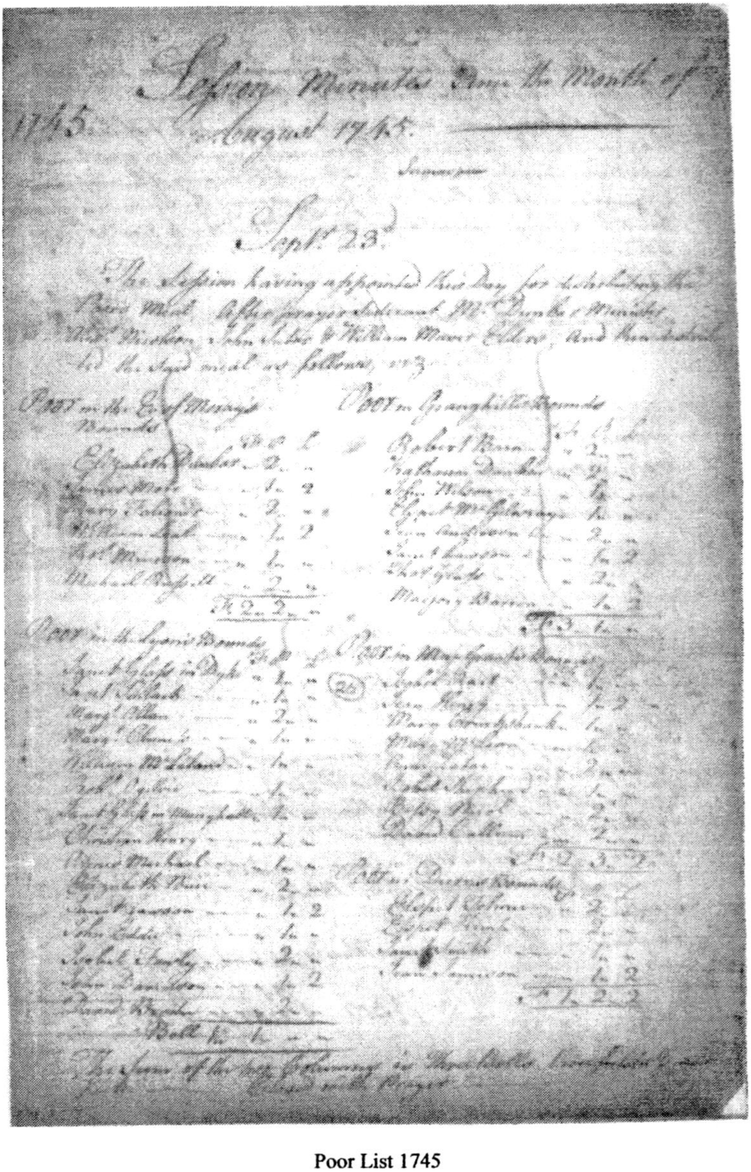
Session Minutes from the Month of
1745. August 1745.

Septr 23.

The Session having appointed this day for distributing the Poors Meal. After prayer sederunt ... and they distributed the said meal as follows, viz

Poor List 1745
National Archives of Scotland CH2/779/5/20

BIBLIOGRAPHY & SOURCES

Sellar. W. D. H.	Moray Province and People	School of Scottish Studies, 1993
Omand. D. (ed)	The Moray Book	Paul Harris, 1976
Cramond. W.	Extracts from the Minutes of the Synod of Moray	Elgin, 1906
Sinclair. (ed)	The Old Statistical Account	1793
	The New Statistical Account	1843
Dunbar-Dunbar. E.	Social Life in Former Days	Edinburgh, 1865
Anon.	A List of those concerned in The Rebellion of 1715	Moray District Archives
Anon.	A List of those concerned in The Rebellion of 1745	Scottish Historical Society, Edinburgh XIII, 1890
Innes C.	Registrum Episcopatus Moraviensis	Edinburgh, 1837
Dunbar-Dunbar. E	Documents Relating to the Province of Moray	Edinburgh, 1895
Douglas R.	The Annals of Forres	Elgin 1920, surviving copy in Forres Library
Shaw. L.	History of the Province of Moray	Glasgow, 1852
Matheson. D.	The Place Names of Elginshire	Stirling, 1905
Simpson. E.	Discovering Moray Banff and Nairn	J. Donald, 1992
Leslie. W.	Survey of the Province of Moray	Elgin, 1793
McDonnell. F.	Sasines for Banff, Elgin etc.	St Andrews, 1996
Watson. J. & W.	Morayshire Described	Elgin, 1868
Rampini. C.	History of Moray and Nairn	Edinburgh, 1897
MacIntosh. H. B.	Pilgrimages in Moray	Elgin, 1924
McKean. C	The District of Moray, An Illustrated Architectural Guide	Edinburgh, 1987
Leslie. W. A.	General View of the Agriculture of Moray and Nairn	Elgin, 1838
Pocock	Tours of Scotland	1760, in NLS
Livingstone, Aikman and Hart	No Quarter Given	Aberdeen University Press 1984
Boece H.	History of Scotland	Aberdeen 1527, using subsequent translations see appropriate footnote
Anon	The Annals of Ulster	
Brodie A.	Diaries of the Lairds of Brodie	National Archives of Scotland
Calderwood D.	History of the Kirk of Scotland	Ed Thomson, T Wodrow Society Edition
Newspapers and Magazines	The Aberdeen Journal The Northern Scot Scottish Forestry Vols 52, 55	
Other Sources	Chartulary of Kinloss Chartulary of Moray	

Forres Burgh Council Minutes
Records of the Presbytery of Forres
NAS Seafield Muniments GD248 various documents
NAS Dunbar of Tarbet and Dunphail papers in GD248
NAS Gordon Castle Muniments GD44 various documents
NAS Gifts and Deposits GD331
NAS Forres Kirk Session Minutes CH2/1448/1 et seq.
NAS RH5/1 et seq, Charters
NAS Exchequer Records, E326 series
NAS Records of Privy Council
NAS Services of Heirs
NAS Index of Testaments, Sheriffdom of Elgin, 18th Century
NAS GD176/1 et seq, Papers of Family of Mackintosh of Mackintosh
NAS E82 series, Exchequer Records, Common Good Accounts
NAS RH1/1 et seq, Miscellaneous Transcripts of Royal Charters
NAS GD94 Papers relating to the Lordship of Urquhart

THE LANDS AND PEOPLE OF MORAY

BRUCE B BISHOP FSA Scot.

A series which studies, Parish by Parish, the History and People of the Baronies, Estates and Lands of Morayshire.
An initial chapter covers the history of each Parish, after which the estates and lands, which were held by various landowners in the parish, are considered individually, from their earliest records up to the time of the first censuses in the mid-nineteenth century.
A chronological list of many of the residents of each estate has been compiled from the Kirk Session Records, Estate Records, Parish Registers, and any other available documentation, together with sketch maps or copies of early plans of each area.

Titles currently available:

Part 1. The Parish of **Elgin** west of the River Lossie, including Inverlochty, Mosstowie, Pittendreich, Manbeen, Auchtertyre, Miltonduff and Pluscarden. 64pp. ISBN 0-9539369-0-2. £4.00
Part 2. The Northern part of the Parish of **Spynie**, including Westfield, Quarrywood, Findrassie, Myreside and Spynie. 66pp. ISBN 0-9539369-1-0. £4.00
Part 3. The Southern part of the Parish of **Spynie**, including Aldroughty, Sheriffmill, Morriston, Borough Briggs and Bishopmill. 54pp. ISBN 0-9539369-2-9. £4.00
Part 4. The Parish of **Elgin** east of the River Lossie, including Thornhill, Clackmarras, Longmorn, Ashgrove, Maisondieu, Bilbohall and Mayne. 60pp. ISBN 0-9539369-5-3. £4.00
Part 5. The Royal Burgh of **Elgin** Prior to 1600, including lists of known residents. 61pp. ISBN 0-9539369-9-6. £4.00
Part 6. The Royal Burgh of **Elgin** in the 17th century, including lists of known residents. 81pp ISBN 0-9542161-0-5. £5.00
Part 7. The Royal Burgh of **Elgin** in the 18th century, including lists of known residents. 73pp. ISBN 0-9542161-1-3. £5.00
Part 8. The Royal Burgh of **Elgin** in the early 19th century, including lists of known residents. 68pp ISBN 0-9542161-2-1. £4.00
Part 9. The North and West of the Parish of **St. Andrews-Lhanbryde**, comprising the former St. Andrews Parish including Kirkhill, Linkwood, Barmuckity and Calcots. 84pp. ISBN 0-9542161-6-4. £5.00
Part 10. The South and East of the Parish of **St. Andrews-Lhanbryde**, comprising the former Langbride Parish including the village of Lhanbryde, Coxton, and Sheriffston. 54pp. ISBN 0-9542161-5-6. £4.00
Part 11. The Eastern Part of the Parish of **Drainie**, comprising Lossiemouth, Stotfield, Kinneddar and Aikenhead. 90pp. ISBN 0-9542161-8-0. £5.00
Part 12. The Western Part of the Parish of **Drainie**, comprising Gordonstoun, Covesea, Ettles, Drainie, Salterhill, etc. 90pp. ISBN 0-9542161-9-9. £5.00
Part 13. The Parish of **Urquhart**, comprising Innes, Leuchars, Urquhart, Cotts, Meft, Maverstoun etc., 88pp. ISBN 0-9546015-0-5. £5.00
Part 14. The Northern part of the Parish of **Speymouth**, including the villages of Garmouth, Essil and Kingston. 64pp. ISBN 0-9546015-2-1. £5.00
Part 15. The Southern part of the Parish of **Speymouth**, including Dipple, Mosstodloch, Stynie Cowfords and Orbliston. 50pp. ISBN 0-9546015-3-X. £4.50
Part 16. The South and West of the Parish of **Bellie**, including Fochabers, Gordon Castle, Bellie Old Church, Bogmoor, Byres, Ordiquish and the southern settlements. 66pp ISBN 0-9546015-5-6. £5.00
Part 17. The North and East of the Parish of **Bellie**, including Spey Bay, Dallachy, Auchenreath, Auchenhalrig, Tynet, Chapelford and the Braes of Enzie. 74pp. ISBN 0-9546015-6-4. £5.00
Part 18. The South and East of the Parish of **Duffus**, including Duffus, Burnside, Shempston, Keam, Unthank and Inchkeil. 84pp ISBN 0-9546015-8-0. £5.00
Part 19. The North and West of the Parish of **Duffus**, including Roseisle, Burghead, Cummingstown and Hopeman. 68pp. ISBN 0-9546015-9-9. £5.00
Part 20. The South and East of the Parish of **Alves**, including Alves, Newton, Ardgye, Cloves etc. 74pp. ISBN 0-9549624-1-9. £5.00
Part 21. The North and West of the Parish of **Alves**, including Earnside, Coltfield, Hempriggs and Milton Brodie. 52pp. ISBN 0-9549624-2-7. £5.00
Part 22. The Parish of **Kinloss**, including Findhorn, Kinloss, Grange and Struthers. 66pp, ISBN 0-9549624-6-X. £5.00

Part 23. The Parish of **Birnie**, including Birnie, Thomshill and Rashcrook, 69pp, ISBN 0-9549624-8-6. £5.00
Part 24. The Parish of **Rafford**, including Burgie, Blervie, Rafford and Altyre, 76pp, ISBN 0-9549624-9-4, £5.00
Part 25. The Parish of **Dallas**, including Dallas, Kellas and Craigmill, 89pp, ISBN 0-9553536-1-0, £5.00
Part 26. The Parish & Burgh of **Forres** prior to 1675, 68pp, ISBN 978-0-9553536-1-0, £5.00
Part 27. The Parish & Burgh of **Forres** 1675 to 1750, 72pp, ISBN 978-0-9553536-5-9, £5.00
Part 28. The Parish & Burgh of **Forres** 1750 to 1800, 72pp, ISBN 978-0-9553536-7-3. £5.00
Part 29. The Parish & Burgh of **Forres** 1800 to 1850, 94pp, ISBN 978-0-9553536-9-6. £5.00

Also in this series:

Witchcraft Trials before the Kirk Session and Presbytery of **Elgin**, 1560-1734. 32pp. ISBN 0-9539369-3-7. £3.00
Population Listings for the Parish of **Dallas**, Morayshire, 1689, 1777 and the 1811 census. Compiled by Bruce B Bishop. 60pp. ISBN 0-9539369-6-1. £4.00
Elgin's Closes. An illustrated study of the Closes and Wynds of the Burgh of Elgin. 68pp. ISBN 0-9542161-3-X. £4.00
Mortcloth Dues and Miscellaneous Death records for the Parishes of **Spynie** (1732-1749, 1755-1760), **Drainie** (1712-1832), **St. Andrews-Lhanbryde** (1632-1837), and Urquhart (1832-1845). Compiled by Bruce B Bishop. 38pp. ISBN 0-9542161-7-2. £3.75.
Population Listings for the Parish of **Knockando**, Morayshire, including 1835 List of Persons in every family in the parish. Compiled by Bruce B Bishop. 48pp. ISBN 0-9549624-0-0, £4.50
Interment Records for the Churchyard of **Knockando**, Morayshire, 1841-1873. 35pp, ISBN 978-0-9553536-6-6 £3.75
A **Moray** Miscellany, some short essays on local history. Bruce B Bishop. 60pp. ISBN 0-9549624-4-3. £4.50
Pre-1855 Death records for the Parishes of **Dyke & Moy** and **Edinkillie**. Compiled by Bruce B Bishop 64pp. ISBN 978-0-9557032-1-8, £4.50

OTHER PUBLICATIONS FROM
J & B BISHOP

It Wisnae me, Mister!. Tales of life as a Prisoner of War during the Second World War, by Charles Muirhead, edited by Bruce B Bishop. 20pp. ISBN 0-9539369-4-5. £2.50
That Celebrated Clipper Ship Vicksburg. London to Melbourne in 1867. William H Haselwood, his journal, edited by Keith L Mitchell FSA Scot. 32pp. ISBN 0-9539369-7-X. £3.00
A Tour in Norway. The 1890 Travel Diary of Christian Carl August Gosch, edited by Keith L Mitchell FSA Scot. 88pp. ISBN 0-9539369-8-8. £5.00
Scottish Population Listings prior to the 1841 census. The Parish of **Dalkeith**, Midlothian, 1811 and 1821 censuses and the 1831 list of Communicants. Compiled by Bruce B Bishop. 84pp. ISBN 0-9542161-4-8. £5.00
Scottish Population Listings prior to the 1841 census. Parish of **Dalkeith**, Midlothian, 1834 Population, CD, £7.50
The History of the Old Church and Churchyard of **Bellie**. Illustrated. Compiled by Bruce B. Bishop for The Friends of Bellie Churchyard. 64pp. ISBN 0-9546015-7-2. £5.00
The Forgotten Tombstones of Moray, Volume 1. The Buried Tombstones of **Dipple**, **Essil** and **St Andrews Kirkhill**. Fully illustrated. 66pp, ISBN 0-9546015-1-3. £5.00.
The Forgotten Tombstones of Moray, Volume 2. The Churchyard of **Old Drainie**, on RAF Lossiemouth now inaccessible to the public, with illustrations and colour photographs. 69pp, ISBN 0-9546015-4-8. £5.99.
The Forgotten Tombstones of Moray, Volume 3. The Buried Tombstones of **Bellie**, **Kinneddar** and **Burghead Old** Churchyards. Fully illustrated. 56pp. ISBN 0-9549624-5-1. £5.99.
The Forgotten Tombstones of Moray, Volume 4, The Buried Tombstones of **Lhanbryde**, **Urquhart** and **Spynie** Churchyards, Fully illustrated. 54pp. ISBN 0-9553536-0-2, £5.99
The Forgotten Tombstones of Moray, Volume 5, The Buried Tombstones of **Alves** Churchyard, Fully illustrated. 82pp. ISBN 978-0-9557032-3-2, £5.99
Monumental Inscriptions, **Bellie** Churchyard and Cemetery. MBGRG, 140pp A4, ISBN 0-553536-2-9, £14.99
Monumental Inscriptions, **Rafford** Churchyard and Cemetery, MBGRG, ISBN 978-0-9553536-3-5, £5.99
Monumental Inscriptions, **Boharm** Churchyard, MBGRG, ISBN 978-0-9553536-8-0, £4.00

All of these Titles may be obtained from
The Aberdeen and North East of Scotland Family History Society, 158 - 164 King Street, Aberdeen
The Scottish Genealogy Society, 15 Victoria Terrace, Edinburgh
J D Yeadon, Booksellers, 32 Commerce Street, Elgin
or they may be ordered direct from the publishers J & B Bishop, Rivendell, Miltonduff, Elgin, Morayshire, IV30 8TJ
adding postage per book as follows;
UK 2nd Class 68p. Europe £1.00p, Rest of the world airmail £2.00
Sterling Cheques or Bank Drafts payable to "Bruce B Bishop".
Prices and Postage Rates correct at 1st September 2007